Ah, Woman!

The Happy Housewife – Lynn Thibodeau

Freedom of Simplicity – Richard J. Foster

The Golden Cow – John White

Ah, Woman!

A new look at old principles... a study of personal accountability for the Christ motivated woman.

GLENDA WALKER

Gospel Advocate Co.
P.O. Box 150
Nashville, TN 37202

To Glenda Faye

AH, WOMAN!

Copyrighted © 1986 by Gospel Advocate Co.

All rights reserved. No part of this publication may be reproduced, stored in a retrieval system, or transmitted in any form or by any means without the prior permission of the publisher.

Published by Gospel Advocate Co.
P.O. Box 150, Nashville, Tn 37202

ISBN 0-89225-286-3

Second Printing—May 1987

Contents

CHAPTER 1

Benevolent Father

As we begin our study of the Christian woman and her related responsibilities, we should get our priorities straight. Perhaps you have already heard or read a great deal pertaining to this subject. But just the same, we're going to discuss it again.

Why? Because most of us know, *logically,* who should be number one in our lives.

> Jesus said unto him, "Thou shalt love the Lord thy God with all thy heart, and with all thy soul, and with all thy mind" (Matthew 22:37, KJV).

However, *emotionally,* we tend to shove our Lord into the deep, dark recesses of our minds, leaving Him there, waiting, until we desperately need His help. Then we call upon Him passionately, with great fear and trembling, begging for His assistance. Unfortunately many of us have never been taught a true, proper image of God.

Some psychologists say that our image of God develops in early childhood from the same image we have of our earthly father. If we were blessed with a loving, gentle father, that image transfers to our impression of God. If, on the other hand, our mortal father was stern and demanding, our image of God will most likely be only of that described in Hebrews 12:29. We will think God is a consuming fire without any feelings of love or tolerance. Sadly, this attitude is usually well-developed in a child at an early age and is not easily changed.

What thoughts come into your mind when you consider the characteristics of God? Do you visualize a kind, pleasant, and benevolent Father who is constantly ready to forgive your every mistake if you are penitent? In John 1:9, we are promised "If we confess our sins, he is faithful and just and will forgive us our sins and purify us from all unrighteousness" (NIV).

Is your God the same God who allowed Enoch to go home with Him without dying? "And Enoch walked with God: and he was not; for God took him" (Genesis 5:24, KJV). Enoch was a very close, personal friend of God's and the Father allowed him to go home to heaven without experiencing death.

Is that your perception of the Father, or do you fit into the category with numerous, tradition-bound Christians who feel that God is someone unapproachable who is to be greatly feared and who would prefer to strike us dead rather than listen to our feeble pleadings?

A Christian woman recently expressed concern over the almost irrational behavior of her husband. She did not know anyone who tried harder to be a servant of God, but he was constantly plagued by "the little things" as she called them. He was always fearful that he would displease God in some small way and erase an entire adult lifetime of service.

God does not deal with His children in this manner. He was the initiator of the plan whereby we can be saved. Granted, God will rain down fire and brimstone on the unjust. This will happen when Jesus comes from heaven with His mighty angels,

> In flaming fire taking vengenance on them that know not God, and that obey not the gospel of our Lord Jesus Christ: Who shall be punished with everlasting destruction from the presence of the Lord and from the glory of his power (II Thessalonians 1:8,9, KJV).

God is not going to do this to His children, but to the unjust.

May our Lord Jesus Christ himself and God our Father, who loved us and by his grace gave us eternal encouragement and good hope, encourage your hearts and strengthen you in every good deed and word (II Thessalonians 2:16-17, NIV).

Does that sound like a father who will strike you down if you stumble? Another thought: have you ever felt that God would be more inclined to listen to you and attend to your needs if you were a man? Many women feel that way. The following story helps to refute that feeling.

In Matthew 14, Jesus was relentlessly pursued by a great throng of people. They followed Him on foot from the towns, and when the evening was approaching, the disciples came to Jesus and said, "This is a remote place, and it's already getting late. Send the crowds away, so they can go to the villages and buy themselves some food" (vs. 15, NIV).

Evidently Jesus had been so busy healing the sick that He had given no thought to the evening meal. But He answered them, "they do not need to go away. You give them something to eat" (vs. 16, NIV).

But the disciples, showing their lack of faith and understanding, and knowing there wasn't enough money to feed the crowd, pleaded that within the mass of people, there were only five loaves of bread and two fish to be found. But as the story unfolds, Jesus took what little food there was and blessed it and the disciples divided it among the people. When everyone had eaten and was filled, the disciples gathered up twelve leftover baskets of broken pieces. (Perhaps one basket for each of the twelve to increase their faith.)

Then Matthew records a beautiful thing: "The number of those who ate was about five thousand men, besides women and children" (NIV).

What were those *women* doing there? Why weren't they home cooking and cleaning house? Why weren't those children bathed and ready for bed? The answer is simple. They had an opportunity to spend some time with the Son of God. Forget the dirty dishes and the piled up laundry! They were going to be with Jesus.

Please don't ever feel that because you are a woman the gospel somehow comes to you second-handedly through a man. Granted, it is not permitted for the woman to hold a public position in the church, but according to Mark 16:15, every creature has a need and a right to hear the gospel and respond to its beautiful message.

If you sense any negativism between yourself and God in reference to His possible harshness or His inclination toward you as a woman, you have missed the whole purpose of why you are on the earth and how much God loves you.

It is most comforting to know that we have a companion who will always listen to us, no matter what the time of day or night. You might hesitate to call even a close friend at three o'clock in the morning, but you need never have to worry about disturbing God's sleep. In Matthew 26, Jesus prayed at night. While His disciples slept, God listened.

Millions of dollars in fees are being spent every year by people who desperately need someone to listen to their problems. God's counseling is free if we will only take advantage of it.

Some people are uncomfortable with prayer. Instead of praying a long, flowing dissertation colored with flowery phrases, simply talk to God in everyday terms. Tell Him plainly what is on your mind. Then think about what you have said for awhile before talking to God again. Prayers of this nature take on the aspect of a conversation and are of great benefit to the one praying. Our bond with God will become much stronger, and it also allows us to work things out of our system and to have a new perspective concerning whatever is troubling us. Problems become clearer because when we have talked it over with God, we have talked it over with the right person.

This type of praying may strike you as a wild, new revolutionary idea, but it's not. This is the exact formula Jesus used when He was in great sorrow in the garden of Gethsemane just before His crucifixion (Matthew 26:36-44).

Surely all of us Christians would admit that our basic goal in life is to be ready for heaven when we die. We profess that we are striving for this and that it is the most important thing in our lives. But sometimes our actions seem to contradict our thoughts.

As an individual living in a sinful world, the only possible way I can be saved is by the grace of God. The blood of Jesus Christ brings me close to God (Hebrews 9:14). If I want to live eternally in glory, this is the only option I have.

God is my Father and He loves me. He wants me to be His child and to serve Him. He is concerned about me and wants me to be saved. ". . . who wants all men to be saved and to come to a knowledge of the truth" (I Timothy 2:4, NIV).

The one thing God wants from me in return is love, and with that love comes obedience. "If you love me, you will obey what I command" (John 14:15, NIV).

God is love (I John 4:8), so we have an excellent teacher. God loved me enough to give His only Son to die in my stead (I John 4:9). Would you give one of your children to die for some drunk who walks the streets or a child molester who haunts a schoolyard looking for some innocent victim? Certainly, I wouldn't, but God is love, and in love He gave His Son.

We must not be lulled into a false sense of security when thinking in terms of our relationship to God. Don't be deceived where God is concerned. He knows our hearts and will not be second in our lives. He only wants first and that is what He will have or He will have nothing.

If anyone comes to me and does not hate his father and mother, his wife and children, his brothers and sister—yes, even his own life—he cannot be my disciple. And anyone who does not carry his cross and follow me cannot be my disciple (Luke 14:26-27, NIV).

We are allowed to have husbands and children, but we had certainly better know that even they cannot come between us and our God. This doesn't mean that we will be perfect and live without sin. We know that we have all sinned and will continue to do so until we die. ". . . for all have sinned and fall short of the glory of God" (Romans 2:23, NIV). But it does mean that we will be honest, with God and with ourselves.

If you are not now serving God with all your heart, make a change. It takes courage to change. You might think that there is no reason to try to reach God, because you will never be able to "make the grade." God is always willing to give His penitent child a second chance. But, no one makes the grade alone. God's grace "curves" the grade in your favor (Ephesians 2:8,9)! God, your benevolent Father, wants you to "finish the course" (II Timothy 4:7), so He gives you an "A"! Keep the faith!

Chapter One

1. Discuss your concept of God. Is your image based upon scripture or myth (tradition)?
2. What are some ways God has shown his love toward us? How are we showing our love and devotion toward him?
3. What are the advantages of being a child of God?
4. What are the consequences if we do not follow God's law?
5. Why is it so important to seal our covenant relationship with our Father?

CHAPTER 2

I Am Woman!

Several years ago the popular recording artist, Helen Reddy, recorded a captivating song with a feminist theme. Although we are hardly feminists, I have borrowed a line from that song for the title of this chapter.

I am woman! Isn't that a wonderful thought? *Woman!* Some women think it is a curse and they wish to be men. But as we have grown in God's knowledge, we understand that to be a woman is a great treasure. A woman is so much more than someone's wife, or mother, or sister, or daughter. A woman is a highly intelligent being created by the supreme Maker.

As women, we have traditionally been bound by two Scriptures in the New Testament. The first is in Ephesians 5:22-24, and says,

> Wives submit yourselves unto your own husbands, as unto the Lord. For the husband is the head of the wife, even as Christ is the head of the church: and he is the Saviour of the body. Therefore as the church is subject unto Christ, so let the wives be to their own husbands in everything (KJV).

The second passage is I Corinthians 14:34:

> Let your women keep silence in the churches: for it is not permitted unto them to speak: but they are commanded to be under obedience, as also saith the law (KJV).

Basically, when I was growing into womanhood, these verses were the foundation of my religious belief. I was to be silent and in subjection, even though I wasn't married.

Of course, these verses are truly applicable to us, but because of their negative emphasis, a great number of women have never learned the positiveness of their own Christianity. In the opening paragraph of this chapter, it was stated that we are not rigid feminists. We are much deeper than that. We are *Christians!* So what is God's purpose for me, a spiritual being, who also happens to be a woman?

All of us at one time or another wonder what we will do with our lives. Those of us who know God try to order our lives after His will. But what is God's will concerning us as women?

Forget anything negative you've even been told about yourself just because you happen to be female. Forget that you are not as strong physically as a man. Forget that you may never be able to compete equally with a man in the business world because of your sex. Instead, we are going to examine woman—a human entity with a soul.

In Genesis, we have the record of the creation of the earth. The crowning glory of this marvelous miracle was the creation of human life, a man and a woman. In Genesis 1:28, the Scripture reads:

> God blessed them and said to them, "Be fruitful and increase in number; fill the earth and subdue it. Rule over the fish of the sea and the birds of the air and over every living creature that moves on the ground" (NIV).

Did you catch it? Go back and read it again. God gave this commandment to both the man and the *woman*. Later in the second chapter of Genesis, we read about the actual creation of the woman, how she was fashioned from a rib taken from Adam's side. It is clear from the very beginning that the woman has been an honored creation of God, put on earth specifically to nurture another human being. In light of this, is it any wonder that woman was chosen to be the loving, supportive wife, the tender mother, the powerful foundation of the home?

When we know—really know—that God's love and grace applies to us as well as to men, we are released from any feelings of inferiority and become more responsive to God and His word. Jesus Christ died for *me*. I am a person ready for a home in heaven. This is my privilege, one that God has given to me because I am a being with a spiritual soul. I am not a second-rate citizen who must fight for equality. Consider these words:

> There is neither Jew nor Greek, there is neither bond nor free, there is neither male nor female: for ye are all one in Christ Jesus (Galatians 3:28 KJV).

I am a child of God. No one can ever take that great treasure away from me. No one.

Therefore, every Christian woman needs to learn to stand on her own two feet before God. When judgment comes, as it surely will, we'll stand before God as individuals.

> For it is written, As I live saith the Lord, ever knee shall bow to me, and every tongue shall confess to God. So then every one of us shall give account of himself to God (Romans 14: 11, 12, KJV).

We will not have our husbands or parents there to tell God what wonderful wives or daughters we were. Our sweet children won't be there to tell God what a wonderful mother we have been. Certainly these acts of kindness will be counted in our favor, but we will stand alone before God, on our own. What a sobering thought!

Therefore, some changes may need to be undertaken before a woman meets God face to face. For one, she must not let her husband make all of her spiritual decisions for her.

It is probable that a number of Christian women are planning their salvation on what their mates are doing. It doesn't matter whether our husband is a minister, an elder, a deacon, a Bible class teacher, or a sinner. What matters is the condition of our own hearts.

In view of this, a woman must plot a righteous course and see that she makes the right decisions in ther personal relationship to God. She must stop putting the wishes of her children before her desire to please her heavenly Father. She must be certain of her own salvation.

We must remember that *before* we are wives, before we are mothers, before we are daughters or sweethearts, we are spiritual beings, one on one with God. If we truly set this truth first in our lives, we will be good wives, good mothers, worthy women, and one day be crowned by the Father Himself.

Mary

We rarely study the woman Mary, the mother of our Lord. Since she has been wrongfully deified by some religious groups, we are hesitant about praising her. But she is a woman worthy of praise and adoration, as are Ruth, Esther, and Dorcas. Their lives all display great courage and a strong love for God.

But let's consider Mary. Here was a young Jewish girl, a virgin living in the town of Nazareth. Most probably, she had very dark skin, black hair, and dark eyes. She was pledged to be married to Joseph, a descendant of David. This couple had a grand future ahead of them.

One day the angel Gabriel appeared to Mary and said, "Greetings, you are highly favored! The Lord is with you" (Luke 1:28, NIV).

Mary was very troubled by the appearance of the angel, but he quickly reassured her. "Do not be afraid, Mary, you have found favor with God" (Luke 1:30, NIV).

I wonder just how prepared Mary was for the next bit of information she was about to receive. She didn't have an inkling of the great purpose her life was about to assume.

> And behold, thou shalt conceive in thy womb, and bring forth a son, and shalt call his name Jesus. He shall be great, and shall be called the Son of the Highest: and the Lord God shall give unto him the throne of his father David: And he shall reign over the house of Jacob for ever: and of his kingdom there shall be no end (Luke 1:31-33, KJV).

Mary evidently possessed the knowledge of conception and was old enough chronologically to conceive a child. However, she had never been with a man sexually, so she could not biologically have a baby. In this passage of Scripture, God gives us a great example to follow. When the time came for His son to be born, He chose a *virgin* from among the women of the world.

Then the angel completed the message:

> The Holy Spirit will come upon you, and the power of the Most High will overshadow you. So the holy one to be born will be called the Son of God. Even Elizabeth your relative is going to have a child in her old age, and she who was said to be barren is in her sixth month. For nothing is impossible with God (Luke 1: 35-37,NIV).

Mary may still have been puzzled and afraid, but she readily accepted the task God had given her. "I am the Lord's servant," Mary answered. "May it be to me as you have said" (Luke 1:38, NIV).

In today's more open and promiscuous society, Mary's pregnancy most likely would have been taken in stride. Perhaps she missed a pill or had an accident. But we are talking about a young, devout Jewish girl, approximately two thousand years ago, who must have felt the tremendous stress and strain of a pregnancy without a husband.

When we consider Mary's plight, it tends to give us a little bit more courage not to worry so much about what others think of us, as long as we are doing the Lord's will.

Mary also had the good fortune to be given a good man. Matthew calls him "a righteous man," and even before Joseph was privy to Mary's wonderful predicament, he sought to divorce her quietly and save her from public disgrace. But soon an angel of the Lord appeared to him in a dream and said,

> Joseph, thou son of David, fear not to take unto thee Mary thy wife: for that which is conceived in her is of the Holy Ghost. And she shall bring forth a son, and thou shalt call his name JESUS: for he shall save his people from their sins (Matthew 1: 20,21, KJV).

So Joseph took Mary as his wife, but did not sleep with her until after the baby boy was born and Joseph called the baby Jesus.

The same courage and faithfulness which guided Mary through her pregnancy and the birth of the son of God also served her well when she later saw that same son die a horrible death by crucifixion. If you have ever lost a child to death, or been close to someone who has, you know that it is one of the worst tragedies a mother must face.

Mary's determination to do God's biding caused her to be chosen for a most wonderful assignment. Truly, "blessed art thou among women" (Luke 1:28, KJV). We should make every effort to follow her example.

Jezebel (I Kings 16)

In contrast to the courageous and righteous woman that Mary portrayed, there is also a dark side to the person woman—a side, which when left unchecked, can produce untold evil. Such a woman was Jezebel. She was so wicked that even now, after thousands of years, no one dares to name a female child after her.

Ahab reigned over Israel as its king for twenty-two years. He was very wicked in his own right, but his evil was magnified when he took for his wife, Jezebel, the daughter of the king of Zidonia. With this marriage came the idol worship of Baal in the temple of Samaria.

Ahab provoked the Lord to anger more than any other king before him. After Ahab married, almighty God, through His servant Elijah the prophet, punished him by causing a great drought to cover the land. During this time Jezebel began killing off the Lord's prophets. But Obadiah, another servant of God, hid one hundred prophets from her.

After a great confrontation between Elijah and the prophets of Baal on Mr. Carmel, Ahab retreated to his palace in Samaria, sullen and angry that God's man prevailed over the men of Baal.

In any marriage, a wife has a great deal of power either to quieten a disgruntled husband or to stir him up to greater anger. Jezebel was quite accomplished at the latter (I Kings 21:25) as we see in the story of Naboth's vineyard in I Kings 21.

There was a vineyard in Jezreel which belonged to a righteous man named Naboth. The vineyard was very close to Ahab's palace, and the king longed to have it for a vegetable garden. So Ahab went to Naboth and pleaded:

> Let me have your vineyard to use for a vegetable garden, since it is close to my palace. In exchange I will give you a better vineyard or, if you prefer, I will pay you whatever it is worth (I Kings, 21:2, NIV).

But the land was Naboth's inheritance from his forefathers and he didn't want to give it up. So Ahab went home, sulked on his bed and refused to eat a bite of food. While the king was acting like a child, Jezebel came and asked him what was wrong. He told her what Naboth had said. Instead of quieting her husband and urging him to forget about the vineyard, she quickly replied, "Is this how you act as king over Israel? Get up and eat! Cheer up. I'll get you the vineyard of Naboth the Jezreelite" (I Kings 21:7, NIV).

The last days of Naboth's life were in the wicked Jezebel's hands. She framed him and commanded that he be stoned to death. Then she told Ahab to take possession of the vineyard for Naboth was no longer alive. Her cunning deceit in evil is as dramatic a lesson to us now as it was to those people long ago. She hated God, scorned and killed His prophets and was determined to have her own way. The manipulation of her husband and the disgrace she brought upon him and herself lives on today.

From these examples, we see that a woman has the capacity to be either good or evil, righteous or wicked. The Lord has blessed my life over the years allowing me to come into contact with some very wonderful, righteous women like Mary. Their lives have enriched mine—guided me when I needed assistance, loved me when I felt alone. But unfortunately, I have also known two who were very wicked. In certain ways, they were like Jezebel. They weren't prostitutes walking the streets for a living, nor were they thieves or lesbians. One even wore the name of Christ. Each in her own way, for some unknown reason, was kind to me, but I knew of the vehemous slander they hurled at others. Their victims lay in heaps upon the ground, cruelly mauled by the wickedness they dished out.

The heinous life of a wicked woman, untouched by the hand of God, is a horrible sight to behold, for nothing is as deadly or dangerous as a woman without love for her fellow human beings. However, our Father in heaven, knowing of our weaknesses, left a beautiful description of what a woman can be if she only tries. Please turn in your Bible to Proverbs 31. Put yourself in the place of the woman in these verses and feel the positiveness of God's love flowing through you.

Chapter Two

1. Are you glad to be a woman? Discuss what is good about your role as woman.
2. Are there disadvantages connected with being a woman? How has the role of the woman in the modern era changed from that of our ancestors?
3. In light of the Women's Liberation Movement, why is it so important for a Christian woman to know her "boundaries" within God's law?
4. Why is it important for a woman to be able to recognize sin?

Chapter 3

The Commitment

If you're married, quickly think back to the day of your wedding. Possibly it was a warm, sunny day in June. You were dressed in a long, white flowing gown of slipper satin with a chapel-length train. The ceremony took place in a large church decorated with mums, gladoli, and long, white tapered candles nestled against a backdrop of palms. Or perhaps you had a smaller wedding at home or before a Justice of the Peace. Your dress was simpler but fit your slender figure beautifully.

The start of a marriage is idealistic—a new home, a promise of two or three healthy, beautiful children, and a husband with a very rosy future.

If you're one of those lucky enough to have enjoyed this sort of idealistic, wedded bliss for many years, then praise God. For the rest of us, the honeymoon has been over for quite sometime. That's not to say we don't love our husbands, for we do. In some respects our unions may have become even stronger enduring the hardships—the ups and downs—of everyday life

According to Webster's dictionary, the word "marry" is defined: "to join (a man) to a woman as her husband, or (a woman) to a man as his wife." The marriage ceremony is the secular application of a biblical matter. "Therefore shall a man leave his father and his mother, and shall cleave unto his wife: and they shall be one flesh" (Genesis 2:24, KJV). This principle is further reinforced in the New Testament. "For this cause shall a man leave father and mother, and shall cleave to his wife: and they twain shall be one flesh" (Matthew 19:5, KJV). Further enhancement of this statute is also found in Mark 10:8.

Why should couples marry in the first place? Why can't humans be like many other members of the animal kingdom, mating with several different spouses at one time?

The reasons for marriage are good ones:

(1) To prevent fornication.

> Flee fornication. Every sin that a man doeth is without the body; but he that committeth fornication sinneth against his own body (I Corinthians 6:18, KJV).

What is fornication? The sexual union between a man and a woman who are not married to each other. This includes adultery. However, God, in His wonderful wisdom, gave us a safe answer for this problem. "Nevertheless, to *avoid* fornication, let every man have his own wife, and let every woman have her own husband (I Corinthians 7:2, KJV).

The sexual union between a man and a woman within marriage is a beautiful, flawless act of love and a strong genetic, biological function. Sexual acts are not something to be endured, but are a bonding fiber of the lives of two people who only love each other and no one else.

Regardless of what the heathenistic world says or does, a Christian cannot participate in the open sexual revolution going on in America today. Not only does God condemn the acts of "lovemaking" (what a terrible disservice we have done to that expression) outside of marriage, fornication is a sin against one s own body. A person would never voluntarily let anyone else harm her body, so why should she consider harming it herself?

(2) To be honorable.

> Marriage is honourable in all, and the bed undefiled: but whoremongers and adulterers God will judge" (Hebrews 13:4, KJV).

The NIV has a beautiful translation of this same verse.

Marriage should be honored by all, and the marriage bed kept *pure,* for God will judge the adulterer and all the sexually immoral.

I love the use of the word "pure" in the Scripture above. It gives marriage a special meaning. A woman who intends to be faithful to her marriage vow can expect, even demand, the same fidelity from her husband. This is the way God intended it to be. It is not impossible for a man or a woman to live up to God's expectations.

Also, marriage provides legitimacy for our children and erases the stigma of disgrace from their name.

(3) To be happy.

God has given us a righteous way to release our sexual desires within the boundaries of marriage. However, marriage encompasses so much more than sex. Let your thoughts once again transcend time to that day when you became a bride. Do you remember the joy and happiness you felt? It was the start of a great, new adventure. Most of us barely had enough money for one person to survive, but somehow we literally existed on love. No problem was so big that the two of us couldn't handle it.

During our first year of marriage, my salary from the Vanderbilt business office was $250.00 a month. My husband was completing his senior year of college and each Sunday we traveled from Nashville to Centerville, Tennessee (a distance of approximately fifty miles), where he worked for the local church and collected $50.00 a week in pay.

One Saturday, we were going to do laundry with $1.25 in our pockets—all the money we had in the world. We had wisely already figured our contribution for the following Sunday. As we started out the front door of our apartment, there on the porch stood the paperboy collecting his monthly fee. We gave him $1.15, and as he left, we collapsed in laughter. We literally had one thin dime left to our name. Why were we able to laugh when we were so broke? *We were in love!* When you're in love, nothing is insurmountable. No problem is too great to solve.

God's wisdom shines through in marriage. We can have love and companionship, a sense of security, someone to lean upon in an hour of trial or disappointment. However, with all the joy a happy marriage brings, there is one thing about marriage many people have failed to remember. *Marriage is a commitment!*

Let's turn back to our Bibles now and read the following verse in Matthew 19:6. "Wherefore, they are no more twain, but one flesh. What therefore God hath joined together, let not man put asunder " (KJV). This thought is so important that it is repeated again in Mark 10:9. "Therefore what God has joined together let man not separate" (NIV).

If you were the bride in a traditional ceremony, you probably remember hearing words similar to these:

"In the presence of God and these witnesses . . .
For richer, for poorer . . .
In sickness and in health . . .
To love, honor and cherish . . .
With this ring I thee wed . . .
Til death do us part."

In our ceremonies of commitment (yours and mine), our first promise was made before God. While invoking His blessing upon our union with the man of our dreams, we promised in God's presence to forsake all others.

Second, the people assembled—our parents, friends, and relatives—heard our promise of undying love, forever, to only one man.

Third, our promise was made to the man standing at our side. He, above all others, had been chosen as our mate—the only object of our love.

And last, our promise was made to ourselves. One thing a woman possesses that she can always count on is her word. Our word was given "till death do us part." If a woman breaks her word, what else does she have of value?

The basic element of commitment is that I will never, never, never, never leave my husband. Not for any reason, no matter what. Our children need to be taught this truth from infancy. Marriage is for life. Young brides in the church need to make this commitment to their marriages at the very beginning, even before the ceremony. If a woman is not willing to make such a commitment, she should never ever marry!

There are numerous Christians struggling with a loveless marriage, or a union filled with hate or indifference. Don't think that you are by yourself if this is your plight. All any of us have ever desired is to be a loving wife and a good mother to our children. Unfortunately, many women are failing in both categories. It's easy to access this failure by looking at the divorce rate in our country and the displaced, unhappy children who are the victims of our failures.

If your marriage is on the verge of crumbling, divorce is not the answer. God hates divorce. "I hate divorce, says the Lord God of Israel" (Malachi 2:16, NIV). God never intended for husbands and wives to leave each other. Jesus plainly teaches in Matthew 19:8-9, that divorce was never God's way of settling a dispute. If we go into marriage, with a subconscious thought of a way of escape out of an unhappy situation, we may well have laid the groundwork for our own divorce. However, if our hearts are set upon making a marriage last, we'll probably be able to weather the storms that assail that union.

The only clear-cut reason for the dissolution of a marriage, and subsequent remarriage in the New Testament is marital unfaithfulness (adultery).

> But I tell you that anyone who divorces his wife, except for marital unfaithfulness, causes her to commit adultery, and anyone who marries a woman so divorced commits adultery (Matthew 5:32, NIV).

The marriage is doomed unless the party guilty of adultery repents. Even if repentance does come, there may be irrevocable damage which the marriage cannot survive (I Corinthians 7:10-11, KJV).

If your marriage is in trouble, you must work very hard to restore the love and trust you once had. There are no easy answers or magic solutions, but you do have one powerful helper on your side—God! Talk to Him. Tell Him how you feel, what the problems are you may be experiencing. There is hope! Set a realistic goal for the future, forget about all the unpleasant things of the past and never give up.

Our lives don't always turn out to be as glamorous as we thought they would be when we were young. That includes marriage. If you're nearing your forties, it pays to look at your life and assess what you have or have not accomplished. The man you married in your twenties is no longer slim. His receding hairline and the wrinkles around his eyes indicate that you are married to an older man. Perhaps the dreams you dreamed together long ago haven't been fulfilled. They may have slipped from your grasp, never to be realized. Sometimes, you might be tempted to seek elsewhere for fulfillment.

But take a good look at the man you married for a moment. In all the years you've been together, has he ever failed to provide food to eat for you and your children? Has he often had to work in an unpleasant environment which he hated, with worldly people, possibly at a less than satisfactory job? Have you constantly picked at him to buy you more things so that you could enjoy a lifestyle you can't afford? What have you done in your marriage to help him ease the tensions in his life?

When couples were dating they held hands with each other. How often do you hold the hand that once meant so much to you? How often do you say, "I love you"?

A good, strong, happy marriage takes hard work. It

doesn't mean that there won't be arguments or disagreements, but when the difficulties do come, they won't be blown so far out of proportion that irreconcilable damage is done to the marriage union.

If your marriage is not exactly what you had expected, sit down with your husband and have a heart to heart talk with him. The main problem threatening every marriage is lack of communication. If you don't talk to your husband and he doesn't talk to you, how can you possibly ever know what is going on in his life or he in yours? Talk to him. Let him know you want to make him happy. And remember the little things you once did for him when you were dating—a funny little card, a telephone call, and unexpected gift laid on the front seat of the car—anything to let him know that he is still king of your heart and lord of your castle. If he loves you (and he probably does), he'll want your happiness and try to help secure the marriage bond.

Chapter Three

1. List the primary reasons for contemplating marriage.
2. Do you have set goals in your marriage? Discuss which ones have and have not been achieved.
3. Using scripture, define the honorable outlines of marriage.
4. If you encounter problems in your marriage to whom do you turn for help?
5. What should we be teaching our children, both sons and daughters, about the commitment to marriage?

CHAPTER 4

The Network

I cant't really recall when it was that I decided my marriage wasn't perfect. We're celebrating our twenty-first anniversary this year, so it must have been about nine or ten years ago.

I had merrily strolled along through life, confident my husband was perfect because he was handsome, talented, and making a good salary. I just knew my two children were tops on anybody's list, and that I had a marriage made in heaven. The reason I could feel so smug about all of this was that I thought I was perfect too.

Then one day I was stopped dead in my tracks when my husband suggested after a rather "insignificant" disagreement, that I had never learned to admit, "I'm wrong. It's my fault."

"You never take the blame for anything," he said.

I knew he'd always been able to take the blame for some mishap or misunderstanding. I can especially recall seeing him do it with older people. I admired his courage in taking on fault, often times when he was totally innocent of any wrongdoing. Reluctantly, I decided to change. Gradually, as I learned to say, "I am wrong," the fences of pride surrounding my life began to fall.

Admitting that your husband and the marriage you share is not perfect has a cleansing effect upon your life. It's no longer necessary to present to others, or to yourself, the idea of perfection. You are freer to be yourself and to serve

God without the cumbersome albatross of perfection hanging about your neck.

We've all known couples who fight and scratch like cats and dogs in private (either the wife or husband eventually tells), but insist upon presenting a sugary sweet, stable relationship to their friends and relatives. It's a form of hypocrisy that churns in one's stomach to think of the wretched lie they are living.

Comparison

The Christian constantly needs to be on guard against comparison in any form, but especially in the marriage arena. Let's face it, our husbands have faults, but so do we. We shouldn't give up on them just because they don't suit our every whim. We, in turn, don't want them to give up on us.

The human tendency is to compare what our husbands have achieved against what someone else's mate has been able to accomplish. This need for comparison causes only further frustration and unnecessary stress. Why can't we, as logical, intelligent women realize that God is working in our lives everyday. All that we have is a blessing and we are indeed fortunate to have a husband to help pay our bills, to feed us and our children, and to protect us?

Duties and Responsibilities

With the marriage vows come certain duties and responsibilities. Both for the husband and for the wife. Some duties are shared, others are designated for the man, while still others are spelled out for the woman. When these responsibilities are clearly defined to the individuals, according to God's holy plan, there are fewer problems within the marriage. It was in this area, the definition of specifics, that I noticed tiny cracks appearing in my own marriage. Once I had solved the basic structure of roles, the tension mounting inside of my own mind began to dissipate.

The Man's Duties

God has set over his children a network of spiritual authority. It begins with Jesus Christ and the Holy Spirit. As we grow in the church, our elders, or shepherds as they are so affectionately called in our congregation, watch in behalf of each person's soul, guiding and leading us into more fruitful paths. In the earthly family, God has placed the husband as the spiritual and physical head of his household.

I do not pretend to understand why God chose to put the male in charge of our family, but God knew that *someone must be in charge*. What would a ship be without a captain? What would an organization be without leadership and authority? The sooner we submit to this commandment of God, the sooner our lives will take on a much calmer ability to deal with our "captain".

> Wives, submit to your husbands as to the Lord. For the husband is the head of the wife as Christ is the head of the church, his body, of which he is the Savior. Now as the church submits to Christ, so also wives should submit to their husbands in everything (Ephesians 5:22-24, NIV).

For those of you who find this commandment difficult, please consider this one thing. God is just, He love us, and in His magnificent wisdom, He decreed this law for a reason. Quite frankly, and speaking from my own personal turmoil with this passage, I really think God gave us this law to put the woman in her place.

There is a part of some women which wants to take charge—to be in command. We are beginning to do it in the marketplace, the universities of our land, and even in the sports world. But there is one place the woman is never to be supreme as long as her husband lives, and that is in the home.

It is the unlearned woman who now asks, "Do you do everything your husband tells you to do?" A response of this nature questions God's authority over our lives. If we are not totally submissive to our husbands, we can become guilty of insubordination in our hearts. Submission is a decision which comes from within the woman's mind, not from the demands of her husband.

Although we must be in submission to our husbands in everything, we must as Christians be careful of one thing. *We must never violate our own consciences*. We must not follow after our husbands, or anyone else for that matter, to do evil. The line on our conscience must be drawn by each individual. I cannot begin to tell you where yours is, but I know where mine is. Pray for strength in this area and God will give it to you.

Not only is the man the head of his home, but it is also his responsibility to provide the living for his family.

> Cursed is the ground because of you; through painful toil you will eat of it all the days of your life. By the sweat of your brow you will eat your food until you return to the ground (Genesis 3:17, 19, NIV).

The apostle Paul wrote much later in the New Testament: "If a man will not work, he shall not eat" (II Thessalonians 3:10, NIV).

Of course, we realize there are exceptions to this due to illness or injury, but if a man is able to work and does not, as Paul wrote to Timothy, "But if any provide not for his own, and specially for those of his own house (kindred), he hath denied the faith, and is worse than an infidel" (I Timothy 5:8, KJV).

At some point in your life, you have probably known of a man whom Paul was portraying in this verse. Such a man would be described by my grandfather as "shiftless, no-account." A woman has a right to expect support from her husband. Paul's condemnation is appropriate as your thoughts imagine the dirty, little faces of children with hunger as a constant companion.

There is also another side to this man. He is the one who does work, but recklessly spends his earnings on some ruthless sort of entertainment. Alcoholism has been the destruction of many families. The man who is addicted to a bottle is of little use to his family as a spiritual head or as a provider of daily needs.

The Woman's Duties

Do you remember the old "Medic" television show from several years ago? It was a show which dealt with medicine and when the description of the doctor was given at the introduction to the program, the following phrase was used:

The eye of an eagle
The heart of a lion
The hand of a woman

"The hand of a woman." The successful Christian woman takes her hand and weaves a network of strong fibers, enveloping her family with strength and love. In the book of Titus, the apostle Paul admonishes the older, more learned women about their behavior so

> . . . that they may teach the young women to be sober, to love their husbands, to love their children, to be discreet, chaste, keepers at home, good, obedient to their own husbands, that the word of God be not blasphemed (Titus 2: 4-5, KJV).

We do not do these things for our own honor, but rather for the glory of God.

A wife and mother should keep her home reasonably clean (or at least picked up). Some families can live with more clutter than others. The dishes should be washed, the carpets vacuumed, the dirty clothes cleaned, and at least one home-cooked meal should be served—on the average of once a week.

Today everything is aluminum covered, microwaved, zip-locked, fast-frozen, and freeze-dried. Dad comes home from work, gobbles down his food, and leaves immediately for one of many committee meetings on which he "volunteered" to serve. The kids pass by the table grabbing their food on the way out to ball practice. Mother is left to eat alone, to do the dishes by herself, and to feed the livestock (which usually includes two cats, a goldfish, and at least one dog).

Christian mothers, if you are tired of this way of living, rise up and say, "No more."

Several years ago, we made a very good rule at our house and we have stuck by it. No ball teams outside of school teams. No little league! Not having to serve dinner in shifts has done a lot for our family life.

In addition to being the keeper of the home, the woman is also the mother. We will study more about this in the next chapter, but giving birth or receiving a child special through adoption is one of the most rewarding things that can happen to a woman.

Joint Duties

In the game of "Marital Pursuit", there seems to be the inevitable desire of men and women for "one-up-manship." It's rare to find a couple who do not complain about each others little quirks to someone outside the family. These complaints would dwindle greatly if husbands and wives were each doing their best toward fulfilling the desires of their mates. We have studied the individual responsibilities of the husband and the wife, so now let's touch on some joint duties.

Companionship and Love

Let the husband render unto the wife due benevolence: and likewise also the wife unto the husband (I Corinthians 7:3, KJV).

The NIV states it this way:

> The husband should fulfill his marital duty to his wife, and likewise the wife to her husband. The wife's body does not belong to her alone but also to her husband. In the same way, the husband's body does not belong to him alone but also to his wife. Do not deprive each other except by mutual consent and for a time, so that you may devote yourselves to prayer. Then come together again so that Satan will not tempt you because of your lack of self-control (I Corinthians 7:3-5, NIV).

The marriage vow figuratively unites the bodies of the male and female into one being. In this spiritual union you are yourself, but in two people. The Ephesian writer said it like this:

> So ought men to love their wives as their own bodies. He that loveth his wife loveth himself. For no man ever yet hateth his own flesh; but nourisheth and cherisheth it, even as the Lord the church (Ephesians 5:28,29, KJV).

If a man loves his wife, nourishes, and cherishes her, their relationship will develop into one of love and devotion. Her submission to him will be complete and their bond will be the foundation of a strong, family unit.

It is from this bond that the mother and father set up the spiritual framework of the family. If the father or mother fails in this duty, the framework will be weakened by that much. So often this task is left to the mother without the father's help, but the commandment is given specifically to the father. "And ye fathers, provoke not your children to wrath: but bring them up in the nurture and admonition of the Lord" (Ephesians 6:4, KJV).

To any unmarried women, heed this warning! How can your husband do his part if he himself is not a Christian? It is a much heavier load if the woman has to rear her children alone, without the help of a Christian father.

There is a certain feeling between a father and his children that a mother cannot grasp, just as there is a certain bond between a mother and her offspring which transcends comprehension. I am reminded of a certain Christian father who was blessed with three children, two older boys and a younger daughter. He and the boys were occupied throughout the year with scouting and scuba diving, but once a year, this father and his daughter went away together for several days, just the two of them. It was a special time—totally theirs. As the mother related this custom to me, I thought about the close relationship that father was building with his teenage daughter. How sad it would be for either parent to miss the special moments with their children as they are growing up.

Crossovers (Dual Careers)

The last category of duties between the husband and the wife is the "crossovers." In this hectic, stress-filled world, we are seeing an ever-increasing number of working women. Earlier, we mentioned that some men, because of illness, cannot support their families. Also, divorce and the death of a husband have propelled many women into the the business world seeking employment. Unfortunately, the main reason for the working mother and wife is the desire by the wife or the husband, or both, to have more and more of this world's pleasantries. We are no longer content to live in small houses, drive older cars, or wear last year's fashions. Some women have gone to work simply to make ends meet.

Some of our friends built on to their house. The addition made the dwelling more spacious and beautiful, but now the woman is trapped into working in order to make the mortgage payments. For many families, the days are long past when they can live on just what the father makes.

Biblically, it is not sinful for a woman to work outside the home. We know that Dorcas was a business woman, as was also Priscilla. But emotionally and physically our families are suffering. It is a fact that men whose wives have attended college and are working outside the home are more than three times as likely to develop heart disease than men whose wives have only a grade school education and do not work (American Journal of Epidemiology, July, 1983). The pressures we put upon ourselves and our loved ones are not always worth the risk.

Along with the crossover of the woman into the working world, must logically come the crossover of the man into the domestic world. There can no longer be "man's work" and "woman's work" if the husband encourages his wife to work outside the home. The time for compromise is *now*.

Pity the man who married a woman who is totally inflexible;
Pity the woman who marries a man who is totally inflexible.

It would have to be a very insensitive man who, allowing his wife to work, did not in turn help with the household chores. On several occasions my husband has offered to help when I felt pressed. He once told me that he would always help, but often he didn't realize I needed it. Your husband may have the same feelings of tenderness if you just let him know your needs and desires.

Some men are especially good cooks. I remember one friend whose husband's dishes were always a big hit at our church suppers. (His mashed potatoes never had lumps.) On one occasion, she was confined to the hospital for surgery. The home ran without a hitch with her husband at the helm, but soon after her return home from the hospital, she was in total charge again. One day I asked her if her husband wasn't still helping with the housework. She explained that he was of great help until her "feet hit the floor", and then he suddenly forgot how to do anything.

Some men actually like to help around the house; some men don't. That also goes for some women. Some men and women are just plain lazy, often treating others outside the family better than their own mates. Many will never be good marriage partners. Not because they can't, but because they won't. A stubborn will is a hard thing to crack, let alone change. Those who are bent upon anger and selfishness may prove too great a match. Selfishness and contempt toward the one we have chosen for our life's companion has no place in a marriage between Christians.

Expectations

We conclude this chapter with one final thought. Don't set standards for your husband that he cannot possibly attain. You know his strengths and his weaknesses better than anyone else. A farmer cannot be expected to behave like a lawyer. Individuals are rarely ever able to live up to what is called the "superman" or "superwoman" image presented so highly by many best selling books. Be extremely careful what you read, gleaning only the things that will help your marriage, not harm it. Consider that your husband is only human. Just as you are not perfect, allow him his imperfections also.

Chapter Four

1. Discuss the network which supports your life.
2. Why is it so important for the Christian not to deal in comparisons?
3. List the positive things you do for your family. Are you guilty of contributing negative blows to those who depend upon you for support?
4. What are some areas in which you and your husband could improve your relationship?
5. What affect does the presence of children have upon the marriage union?

CHAPTER 5

I Never Knew It Was Going To Be Like This!

Take a quick look at the following schedule. Does it remind you of anyone you know?

6:00 A.M.—Jump out of bed, put on the same clothes you wore yesterday. You'll shower and change later.

6:15 A.M.—Fix breakfast, first for your twelve-year-old son, then a different breakfast for your daughter who had to shower in the morning so that her hair would be fresh and clean; then a third breakfast for your husband who said he didn't want to eat but then changed his mind.

7:15 A.M.—Rush everyone out of the door, grab your keys and purse and dash off to school, hoping the kids won't be late. (You're lucky if you live in a school district with bus service.)

8:00 A.M.—Return home, watch the morning news on TV while washing dirty dishes.

9:00 A.M.—The rest of the day can be spent in a million different fun ways: washing dirty tennis shoes, cleaning the toilets (Oh! the joy of having more than one bathroom); chasing the neighbors' animals out of your favorite flower beds; getting dressed just in time to sneak in the back of Ladies Bible Class (you have a run in your hose but can't do anything about it now); volunteering at school; or sewing, baking (do mothers do that anymore?) Just before you pick the kids up at school, drop by the post office and buy six stamps (only six because that $5.00 bill has to last until Friday and it's only Monday); stop by the market for extra milk (the twelve-year-old emptied most of the carton last night—that five is dwindling fast.)

3:30 P.M.—Pick up kids at school, run to piano, or the dentist, or soccer, or football, or baseball practice (take your pick).

Then home to prepare dinner, more dishes to wash, baths to give, and not even enough time to watch your favorite one hour television show. When you are finally ready to collapse in bed after a good hot shower, a voice, usually female, comes to you from down the hall, "Mother, I have to have clean jeans by in the morning." You just want to scream!

Does this sound like a typical day in your life? Add to this crazy, hectic schedule the fact that over 65% of mothers with school age children now have jobs outside the home. So all of these things still have to be done, only after hours. Sometimes, it is even convenient to have a "job" so that you use it for an excuse not to clutter up your days with so many other activities.

Being a wife and a mother is one of the most energetic and exhausting responsibilities a woman can have. When you first marry, you don't have the slightest idea of the strength you'll be called upon to display in the years ahead. We love our families and would honestly not trade our husbands or children for anyone else's. There may be a few exceptions to this, but generally we are satisfied with the family God has given us. But let's face it. We live in a society that's moving at breakneck speed, and if you're not inclined to move along with it, you soon become an oddity. The world just isn't the same today as it was when our mothers were rearing us. Modern appliances and inventions have freed us from so many chores of drudgery. Now we have, as wives and mothers, more "spare" time in which to branch out and expand our lives. Often what we deem progress may not be progress at all.

Consider # 1:

There is a definite advantage in a person's life when she is subjected to hard work. Not only is her body more apt to be physically fit, building strength and endurance, but the releasing of anxiety is often done during the course of vigorous, sustained activity. Even though we love our automatic washers and dryers, countless frustrations were no doubt banged out on the old scrub board of long ago.

Consider # 2:

The realization of more uncommitted time has left scores of women at a loss with what to do with themselves. This in itself has led many women to work outside the home. A great deal of pressure has been put upon the American woman not to waste time. Thus to fill any spare moment which could have been spent even in worthwhile leisure activity, we are compelled to work, work, work. Approximately 33% of the American work force is women. We are finally making our mark in the world, but at what price?

I remember walking home from school every afternoon as a child, knocking on the screen door of our house, and calling for my mother. If she wasn't there, I became upset. But she was there, and I could always count on that. I was secure in the fact that she would always be there, unless there was an emergency.

There is a new phenomenon sweeping America today called "the latchkey kids." These are the children of working mothers. They usually leave the house in the morning after their mothers go to work and return in the afternoon before their mothers come home. Many of these children suffer multiple fears brought about by being forced to enter an empty, lonely house by themselves. Many are very young, possibly even pre-schoolers. The mothers who are channelled by need into day-care facilities often find them unsuitable for their children. It has become a tragedy in America that as mothers we aren't allowed to do much mothering anymore.

As we discussed in the previous chapter, there are circumstances when a mother must work outside her home as a result of illness to her husband, or the loss of his job. It also could be that the mother is divorced or widowed and is forced to work to support herself and her children. There could also be the added burden of caring for elderly parents which creates an additional strain upon the family's finances. Quite possibly your husband's job does not pay enough to allow the family to sustain a decent lifestyle. And, finally, there are women who simply want to work. They like the idea of a career, holding down an important or lucrative position. Some women are much better organized and happier when away from their houses and domestic demands.

The Scriptures say that a married women must be a keeper of the home (Titus 2:4,5). If she can do this and still maintain an outside job, then it is not wrong for her to do so. However, we must all remember that our first and most important responsibility is to our husbands and our children. When we took our marriage vows, we promised in effect that we would see to the needs of our mates and to any children which might follow from the union. This has to be our *primary* goal. Anything which keeps us from fulfilling that goal must be wrong.

Another note here. Many Christian women still think that it's wrong for women to work for money. These women, nevertheless, fill their extra time with numerous social and volunteer activities which take them away from the responsibility to mother. What is the difference whether or not you're getting paid, if you're never home when you're needed?

A working mother must be honest. Are you working because you want to work, to have a nice home, a new car, pretty clothes, or are you working because of necessity?

One lady was constantly heard to say that all she wanted was to *be able* to quit work, stay home and be just a plain housewife. However, she and her husband had recently built a beautiful new home (they owned quite a nice house to begin with), bought a new car, and the family was always dressed immaculately. Even though her words said one thing, it was obvious she wanted other things more than staying home. I honestly do not think she realized her predicament. While teaching this particular point in class one time, a lady remarked, "If I don't work, we lose our house." At least she knew why she was working.

Many of us worked before our husbands made enough money and before our children were born. At that time in our young married lives, it usually took both salaries to pay the bills and buy the groceries. Unfortunately, as our husbands' salaries increased, so did our lifestyles. It has always taken a very wise person to live within her means. However, in plastic America, the correct password is charge, charge, charge and debt, debt, debt.

There is an old adage: the more money you make, the more you spend. So often this is the case. With more money comes the feeling of more power and more freedom. If the ability to produce more money isn't coupled with good sense and proper planning, the increase of debt and poor management can do nothing but put a strain on one's personal relationships.

A Christian counselor on money management held a seminar in Huntsville, Alabama, which I attended. At first, I was reluctant to enter the room, knowing that crossing the threshold of that doorway would instantly label me as a "poor credit risk." To my surprise, every chair in the room was taken, with people standing in every available space. A doctor and his wife were very close to the front, with aerospace engineers, secretaries, and business men from nearly every walk of life. Immediately, I felt a comradeship with these people, cognizant of the fact that nearly all of us, regardless of income, have money problems and financial worries.

Many women work because they sense a need to help support the family. We feel obligated to help our husbands bear the burden of earning a living. But this is not the woman's responsibility. It has always been the husband's obligation to provide for the family.

A very dear friend who has raised four children (one mentally handicapped) to adulthood, kept her elderly mother and father-in-law until their deaths, and maintained an active Christian existence. She once said to me, "I let my husband support our family. After all, that's his job. I take care of all this other stuff." What a wise woman! She doesn't wear the latest fashions or have a lot of gold jewelry adorning her neck and fingers, but she is happy and content.

The need to possess money and to be less dependent upon their husbands for money has also plunged many women into working. But what happens when the wife becomes too independent of her husband? We should never lose sight of the fact that our husband is the head of our home, and that we are to enhance his position as the leader of the family. If a woman ever feels, because of the satisfaction of her job or the money she makes, that she can undermine her husband's position, she is headed for trouble. There is something in the make-up of the man which makes him dominant. He is the leader. The woman cannot take that authority from him and continue to have a blissful marriage.

In Luke 12:15 Jesus said, "Take heed and beware of covetousness: for a man's life consisteth not in the abundance of the things which he possesseth" (KJV). The NIV says, "Watch out! Be on your guard against all kinds of greed; a man's life does not consist in the abundance of his possessions."

Somehow, we have come to think that a man's or a woman's importance has to do with what he or she has accumulated in earthly goods. This could not be further from the truth. Think for a moment about the rich people you have seen—the ones whose pictures appear repeatedly in newspapers and magazines. How many of these people are Christians? Are any of them devoted to our Lord? I'm afraid the answer is "not very many." However, they are the ones considered successful by the world. And, if we are truthful, they are also the ones we consider successful.

We must not, as Christians, fall into this trap of Satan. Our life cannot be bound up in the new sofa we have just purchased or in the exclusive membership of a club we have just bought so that we can swim in the pool once or twice a week. This is success according to the world, but not according to God.

Many women have built their self-esteem upon a good job. No doubt a well-paying position can do wonders for a person's self-image. But the image you have of yourself comes from within. It does not hinge upon what others think of you, only what you think of yourself. If it takes a job to produce a good self-image, what happens if you move or get laid off and you no longer have your employment?

The best self-image a wife and mother can have comes from the work of God. When you realize that *you* matter, just as you are with no frills, when you understand that you're a child of God, created in His image by love, and that He'll take care of you, then a healthy self-esteem begins to grow.

We have become so concerned with having a comfortable house and financial security for the future that we forget that God is taking care of us, no matter what happens. God took care of our parents before us and He'll take care of our children after we're gone. We must have faith in Him to do this for us as He promised He will.

Now getting back to that schedule at the first of the chapter. Did you notice that the woman allowed no time for herself? She also didn't allow very much for God, did she?

You may be a good mother, always there when your children need you. You may also be helping your husband in countless ways, all of which are working to strengthen your marriage. But, if you are neglecting yourself along the way, you are robbing your family or what you could be. We musn't continually look back at what we have been or what we've accomplished in the past. Instead, we must look forward and see in what direction we are headed, and how we can improve ourselves physically, mentally, and most of all, spiritually.

Later, in another chapter, we will deal at length with our body but for now we will just touch upon the spiritual.

If you are constantly in a hurry, short tempered because things aren't done on schedule, yelling and screaming at your family, then you are not being a very good mother to your children or a very good mate for your husband. One of the hardest things for a woman to do is to take time for herself, but you must do it. The "superwoman" complex in all of us urges that we must go on and do more and more things, and never stop. This is a myth! Let the dirty dishes go for awhile, sit down and prop up your feet. (And don't feel guilty!) Learn to relax. Practice talking to your Father in heaven. Take time out everyday for a period, however brief, of meditation and study of God's word. There is great comfort to be found there.

Chapter Five

1. Discuss some ways in which we could make our lives a little easier.
2. Make a list of things you do not like about your daily schedule. Within the next year try to work out a way to delete them if they are not absolutely necessary.

3. What are some positive aspects of a woman working outside the home? Some negative?
4. List ways in which women in the church can help their sisters in Christ who find it necessary to work.
5. What does our self-esteem have to do with the way we conduct our lives.

CHAPTER 6

Now, On To The Children. . . . .

She was tiny and pink, her small eyes accented by large brows which was characteristic of her father's family. The nurse laid her beside me in the hospital bed. My first born—flesh of my flesh—delivered from my womb, a child conceived during a union of love.

The birth of a child is the most personal event a woman can ever experience. Although shrouded in pain, the mother endures labor, hoping with proper expectation for a live birth. When this occurs, the pain is forgotten—joy and happiness envelope the family.

> A woman when she is in travail hath sorrow, because her hour is come: but as soon as she is delivered of a child she remembereth no more the anguish, for joy that a man is born into the world (John 16:21, KJV).

Many things are bound to change throughout my lifetime, but one thing will never change. I am the *mother* of Marnie Elizabeth Walker. That one unchangeable fact brings a great deal of pride to my life. My child, my offspring, will carry on for me in the future.

When couples marry, if a natural course follows, the marriage will be blessed with children. It is what most of us desire. We pray for a child. Hopefully, the children will be normal, born without deformity or handicap. However, if the children born to a union are not wholly well, whether physically or mentally, the parents must make certain instant and long-range adjustments. Every mother is relieved after delivery to hear the doctor describe a healthy child. However, we try to prepare ourselves during the nine months of pregnancy for any complication which might arise.

A most courageous couple was blessed with two daughters. The first was about two years old when the mother discovered she was pregnant with her second child. Before long, the parents began to notice progressive deterioration in the behavior and mannerisms of their daughter. Within a few months, the once healthy toddler was horribly deformed and mentally destroyed by a very rare disease. The doctors informed them she would not live much past the age of six years, but the child lived to be seventeen. They were desperately afraid that the disease which afflicted the first child would also claim the second, so more years of torturous waiting finally resulted in the knowledge that the second little girl had been spared.

Why was this couple "blessed" to have a child who had to be hand fed, whose little body had to be carried around from place to place by her parents, and for years had to be changed just like a small infant?

First let me ask another question. If one of your own children was born healthy and for two years crawled and walked around doing all the things a little one is supposed to do, what would you do with that child who was so much a part of your life, if suddenly she were taken ill, never to recover? You'd immediately summon the very best medical help available, nursing and caring for your child, nurturing and praying for her recovery. That's exactly what this mother did. And it was this love and care which prolonged her daughter's life. The mother became an expert at treating uncontrollable diarrhea and at handling the unkind, ridiculous remarks of the ignorant. This couple truly was blessed and will forever hold the memory of their little girl dear in their hearts.

Right now, wherever you are, thank God for your healthy, active children!

Some couples do not desire children and, if this is their feeling, they are very wise never to pursue parenthood. Then there are the couples who want desperately to have children, but biologically cannot produce one. Perhaps their personal agony can be relieved through adoption, but now there are fewer babies than ever available by this means.

(A special note to the women who have children concerning the women who do not have children. *Lay off!* Just because you're married and have kids, please don't assume you know everything about life. Some of the shallowest women in the world are those who only know of diapers, dirty laundry, school bake sales, and who never read.)

But supposing that after awhile little ones are born into your family. Your life will never be the same again. Not only will the condition of your heart be changed (a little child can work wonders on the hardest of hearts), your daily schedule and lifestyle will now revolve around the baby, its needs and its demands. As the child matures, you will be able to mold its behavior in such a way that the child will become a meaningful part of the family. It is this early shaping of a child's life which is so important to it in later life. We like to think that it is mainly for our benefit that our children are well-behaved and responsive to the needs of others. However, the person who benefits most is the child growing into a healthy, well-balanced, and spiritual individual.

There are so many bad things written and said about children—especially teenagers—living in the world today. They are said to be rebellious, lazy, coke-freaks, and delinquents. Our public and private schools run rampant with drugs and knives. And, of course, whenever any tragedy occurs, the media blasts it all over the television screen and the front pages of our newspapers.

Today our children are faced with many different kinds of temptations we did not have to face as kids. Drugs are everywhere, and even children in elementary school, can buy drugs if they want to. Immorality, especially sexual immorality, is lurking in every shadow. Lying, cheating, and stealing are all readily accomplished traits.

Now that we know it is out there, let's look at our children—the children of Christian parents. Our influence, the fact that we have Jesus Christ and the Holy Spirit dwelling within us (I John 4:13 and I Corinthians 3:16), should make a difference in their lives. How do I know this? Because it made a difference in my life to be taught by spiritual parents, just as it did in Timothy's. Therefore, it should make a difference in my own children's lives. That is, if I am doing my job.

When I was a teenager, it was a big deal to go out and get drunk—to park and "make out." This term carries with it varying degrees of intensity, but to some classmates it meant "fornication." Smoking was also a big challenge to be met, as was dancing.

The year after I left high school, two boys, one year younger than myself and whom I had casually known, attended the Harvest Ball on the Wednesday night before Thanksgiving in the school gym. They were drinking heavily and decided to go out and rob a filling station. While there, they pumped nine bullets into the attendant's body even though he was cooperating with them. After throwing their guns off a bridge into the river below, they returned to the dance as if nothing had happened. Only a chance remark overheard by an underclassman and related to his mother ever brought about their arrest.

As much as we hate the idea, there are mean people in the world. They were living when we were growing up and they are still prowling the earth today. We may call them misguided, disillusioned, down-trodden, or ill, but they are separated from God and we *must not* let their influence for evil be greater upon our children than our influence for good.

For some inexplicable reason, many parents melt in the face of a fourteen-year-old girl throwing a temper tantrum.

"All of my friends are going (doing, wearing) so why can't I?" Parents repeatedly give their teenage boys money, and then have no supervision over how they spend that money, whether it be on bubblegum or liquor.

Have you ever stopped to consider whether or nor those children sitting on Jesus' lap in Mark 10:14 ever went through the "terrible two's"? They may have, but I bet they didn't display those tendencies of "bratism" for very long. Why? Because they were the children of Jewish parents.

> If a man have a stubborn and rebellious son, which will not obey the voice of his father, or the voice of his mother, and that when they have chastened him, will not hearken unto them: Then shall his father and his mother lay hold on him, and bring him out unto the elders of his city, and unto the gate of his place: And they shall say unto the elders of his city, This our son is stubborn and rebellious, he will not obey our voice; he is a glutton and a drunkard. And all the men of his city shall stone him with stones, that he die: so shalt thou put evil away from among you: and all Israel shall hear and fear" (Deuteronomy 21:18-21, KJV).

When Sam David Tatum, a Christian man and juvenile court judge of Davidson County in Nashville, was sitting on the bench, there were rarely, if ever, any Jewish children brought before him for delinquency, in spite of the fact that Nashville had a very large Jewish community. If the Jewish parents, without the help of Jesus Christ, can raise their children to be responsible and obedient, just think what we can do with His help.

There are several different stages in children's lives. Sometimes, they can be sweet, and they can be hateful, rebellious, and stubborn. (Of course, as their parents, we have never displayed any of these traits and wonder where in the world they got them.) However, the trouble is not with most children, but with their parents.

Parents simply tend to lose their backbone when it comes to dealing with their children. They are somehow afraid of damaging their children's emotional stability if they display signs of force. Also, some parents are afraid of losing their children's love. Why else would a mother tolerate a son or daughter slapping her face or refusing to even help bring the groceries into the house from the car? Just the other day it was related to me how one of the teenage girls in our local congregation snapped orders to her mother, "Bring me a drink," without even a "Please." Sadly, the mother did it. Incidently, all of these rank displays of rebellion and arrogance happened in Christian homes.

Successful parenting is active and aggressive. It shows interest and concern for the child's well-being. Just as you would not stand by and watch your small child pick up a hot coal from an open fireplace, you must not idly stand by and let Satan lead your child into sin.

Here are some positive steps to help in the nurturing of our children.

(1) Children should be *loved*.

A teenage girl had occasion to visit my daughter once in our apartment. She had failed to tell her parents where she would be, and her father was frantically searching the streets and the nearby convenience stores with no success. After about thirty minutes, my daughter accompanied the girl back to her apartment, and the father was overjoyed to see his daughter safe and alive. However, he was very angry with her for causing him so much anguish. As she entered the apartment, he gave her a sudden, swift kick in the seat. Some of us have very strange ways of showing our love.

"But I do love my children," you profess. But do *they* know it? When our children are little, it is very easy for us to hold them and cuddle them while they sit on our laps. But what about after they are older, when they become teenagers, and even college age? It is heart-warming to see grown men hug their fathers. Even married children still need love and encouragement from their parents.

This love is not connected to any deeds our children might perform. This love is like the love we have from God, a graceful love, given to a child simply because it is our child, not good or bad, just our child. This love lets your teenage son know that you'll be there, loving him, no matter what. This love is free.

(2) Children should be *disciplined.*

Many parents are against any sort of physical punishment for a child. Let's see what the Scriptures say.

He who spares the rod hates his son, but he who loves him is careful to discipline him (Proverbs 13:24, NIV).

Do not withhold discipline from a child: if you punish him with the rod, he will not die. Punish him with the rod and save his soul from death (Proverbs 23:13,14, NIV).

Folly is bound up in the heart of a child, but the rod of discipline will drive it far from him (Proverbs 22:15, NIV).

Enough said? These are the principles those Jewish parents used in rearing their children. Remember also, that all correction is to be administered with love, not anger.

There are two men who have helped me considerably in the growth of my own children. The first is Dr. James Dobson in his book *Dare to Discipline.* This book is absolutely the best when it comes to helping parents sort out their problems in dealing with kids. He covers every aspect of parenting with simple, honest teaching based upon God's word.

The other advice came from Tim Walker, who for almost eighteen years ministered to youth. He is the author of a book for teens entitled *Christian Living Is for Real.* He, incidently, happens to be my husband. His instructions to parents: "Don't make too many rules for your children. Have a few, simple rules, easily understood and easily followed. Talk them over with your children, be sure they are clearly defined and well-understood. Then actively see that those rules are followed. If you have promised a certain punishment for the breaking of a certain rule, then, if it is the last thing you ever do, carry out that punishment. Don't make threats or promises unless you plan to carry them out." One thing a child picks up on quickly is your ability or inability to keep your word.

(3) Children should be taught to accept *responsibility*.

Responsibility has to be learned from an early age, and usually it begins with something as simple as a child picking up toys. As they progress, little ones can be taught to dress themselves, make their beds, and keep their rooms straight. Often this training is forgotten by age fifteen. However, this is the fault of the parent, especially the father, and not the child. (Mothers, if you're having trouble with your teenagers about their dirty rooms, send dad in to have a few words with them.)

Our children must know that they are responsible for their own actions. It is sad for a parent to continually bail children out of mischief, whether it be at school or in the neighborhood. It would probably be wise to let them suffer through the consequences of their actions once or twice. If your child is constantly in trouble with his teachers or the police, it is way past time to take an objective look at his or her character. You are building that child's credibility for the future and lessons need to be learned now.

(4) Children should be made to *work*.

Adults dream of the day when the *Reader's Digest* Sweepstakes letter will come to their house informing them of a lifetime income of $100,000 a year. No more work. Kids are the same. Why should they be working when they could be off under their beds daydreaming about deep, dark cavernous tunnels with monsters, girls, cars, boys, or make-up? Besides, we'll buy them anything they want anyway.

Unfortunately, it is a fact of life that we must all work. Children should start early doing easy chores around the house, emptying trash baskets, clearing the table, keeping their rooms straight, hanging up their clothes. They aren't working because we need their help so much. They are working to learn skills, promote self-esteem, to have a good feeling about being able to accomplish something. Hopefully, when they are older, they are able to look at a harder job and successfully carry it out to a conclusion.

A male child should be actively taught by caring parents that when he is grown he will have to support himself and then a family if he marries. Likewise, a young girl should be taught that she will have to take care of a home, a husband, and children if she marries. You might be appalled at the number of young couples who marry, neither one having brought proper skills to the union. We are failing our children when this happens.

Surely, it is obvious by now that our children need an aggressive, positive atmosphere in which to grow into adulthood. This cannot be left to chance. The sinister devil is at work in the world, and we must guard our children from this heinous power who would corrupt them. Our children are assailed with wickedness on every hand, but especially in the areas of drug abuse and sexual immorality.

Do not be deceived! Drugs are everywhere. Just because you have not seen them does not mean they don't exist. The drug culture is sweeping America, but it does not have to claim our children as victims. Unfortunately, parents haven't always set a good example for their children. The use of alcohol has become so common in our society, that the idea of condemning it is humorous even to religious people. If your drink even socially, your child has easy access to this most damning drug. The use of pills to acquire a high, a low, or stability on one's life is on the increase. But sadly, not only on the streets, but also in the medical profession. Doctors are among the chief abusers of drugs, and so are some of their patients. When a friend's mother died, almost immediately he was offered Valium by three different people.

The actor Michael Landon has always exhibited a keen interest as a parent in the lives of his children. He has performed a momumental service to America in the production of a very decent show for viewing in his "Little House on the Prairie." While attending a drug seminar, an interviewer asked him how parents could help their own children in dealing with the current drug problem. He answered, "Don't let your children use drugs. Keep them from doing it." The statement sounded silly for a moment, but following closer examination his words began to make sense.

Don't give your children money if you suspect they are using it to purchase drugs. As a parent you are in charge of your children's lives, at least in most states, until they are eighteen years of age. If you have to physically restrain them, keep your children away from the drug users and sellers. Seek professional help, even if it means incarceration in a hospital or institution specially equipped to handle drug abuse. Don't sit by and let the problem drag on and on. Be in charge, be aggressive, find help. And don't ever give up on a child. Give your children a good foundation built upon Jesus Christ and they won't need drugs. Drugs are a way of escaping, but if they have a positive base, something to hang on to that's worth hanging on to, they'll be able to resist the temptations or peer pressure for peer acceptance.

Remember that as a child matures there is bound to be a lot of natural curiosity about sexual development. Try to be as frank and honest as possible in dealing with this subject. Start when the child is very young about small things. It gets easier as you go along.

Start by teaching your children that they were made in the image of God and that their bodies are special. When children reach the teen years, they should have a clear understanding that sexual intercourse (fornication) outside of marriage is forbidden by God's law (I Corinthians 6:9,10,KJV). No matter what your teenager tells you, whether about themselves or a friend, do not appear shocked. Stay calm, think carefully about your answer. Children need guidance. They will falter at times. We should be there with love and encouragement to lift them up when the mistakes happen.

Over the years we've tried to fill the void in our children's lives by exposing them to everything from sports to music to literature—searching vainly for a hero figure for them to emulate and follow. Although an avid sports fan myself, sports is not the answer.

In the August 15, 1983, issue of *Sports Illustrated,* Robert Alto, the team physician for the Golden State Warriors is quoted as saying, "I agree that 75% of the NBA has used it (cocaine)." Orthodontist Dr. Billy Cannon, a two time All-American and Heisman Trophy winner from LSU has been sentenced to five years in prison and fined $10,000 for his part in a $6 million dollar counterfeiting scheme. Our sports figures are being charged with everything from possession of drugs to rape. Even though we still have numerous athletes of the stature of Merlin Olsen and Carl Lewis, the negative vibes coming from the sports world are crushing the faith of young people everywhere. It is not uncommon to learn that leading actors, actresses, and popular singers are homosexual and/or bisexual. The movies and books presented to our children for their age group are filled with soft pornography and nudity enticing their innocent young minds toward corruption. Mothers, have you viewed a PG-13 movie lately?

It is time for parents to take a stand against evil. A problem has the potential of either destroying a person or making one stronger. We must begin to instill within our children that strength which is only found in Jesus Christ. What a hero! He *died* for the people He loved. He not only gave His life for the people of His country but for the whole world. He was tempted just as our children are and will continue to be.

> For we do not have a high priest who is unable to sympathize with our weaknesses, but we have one who has been tempted in every way, just as we are, yet was without sin. Let us then approach the throne of grace with confidence, so that we may receive mercy and find grace to help us in our time of need (Hebrews 4:15, 16, NIV).

Don't kid yourself. There were evil women who would have gladly ensnared our Lord in fornication. The Pharisees accused him of all sorts of wickedness, but what a marvelous example He was to us and to our children. Make Him come alive for them. Let them see His loving kindness and bravery in your life. Make Him a hero to them. He is their only real hope.

Chapter Six

1. What role do children play in our lives?
2. If you were unable to have a child by natural childbirth, to what lengths would you go in order to have a child? How do these concur with God's law?
3. Why is it important for parents to be aggressive in parenting their children?
4. What role does "common sense" play in the rearing of our children? Can good kids be produced without reading books on psychology?
5. Discuss the "heroes" influencing your child's life.

CHAPTER 7

The List

Right now, before you do anything else (don't even turn the page), take a pen and paper and list the twenty-five most important things in your life. A beautiful ring left to you by your mother, a favorite book, a precious memory, your children. Whatever. There's no trick involved. Just remember, these are things important to you, not anyone else. After you've written out your list take a few seconds to arrange it in order of importance, if you like, although it's not necessary. Your time limit is ten minutes. When you have finished your list, you may turn the page.

It might be interesting to compare your list with that of a friend or a neighbor. Possibly there are things on your list which might not appear on your best friend's or even your husband's. But for now, tuck your list away until later.

From the very beginning of this book, we have dealt with our relationship to God, and our inherent responsibility toward Him. God is our creator and unless we are foolish like the man in Psalms 14:1, we know that. "The fool hath said in his heart, There is no God" (KJV). The same thought is repeated again in Psalms 53:1. Whenever something appears twice in the Scriptures, it's best to take a second look.

However, your belief in God is evident. Otherwise, why would you be reading this book? What is not evident in many of the writings for women today is *the real reason anything matters in the first place.*

Everything about God is ethereal—beyond man's real

comprehension. The fact that God has no beginning and no end, that He sits on a throne in a place called heaven—a city with streets of pure gold as transparent as glass where there will be no death, no tears, nor pain—cannot possibly be understood by a mere human being. But it is through our humanity, purely from a physical point of view that we can really grasp God's great gift to us. Only by our intermingling with each other, giving of our love to someone else, receiving love from one another, by being human can we understand the love of God for man. Even though God has done countless good things for His people, beginning with Abraham, then on to his descendents, to the Israelites, and finally to the Gentiles, the love of God toward His people was ultimately shown in one unsurpassed deed of time.

Nicodemus (John 3)

Late one night a Pharisee named Nicodemus came to see Jesus. He was a very influential man, a member of the Jewish ruling council. He may have come at night out of fear of the Jews or to avoid the large crowds always surrounding our Lord. Whatever the reason, Nicodemus was convinced Jesus was a teacher from God because he knew only a man of God could perform such miracles as were being done.

It is interesting that only John records this account of the meeting for out of this discussion comes the most powerful knowledge a woman can possess. You may have the ability to earn a docorate from Harvard, become vice-president of your firm, or hold a position on the board of directors of a large bank, but you will never hear anything more profound or important than what Jesus said to Nicodemus that night long ago. And this powerful knowledge is not contained in the discourse between the two on the necessity of being born again, although that is very important. The simple magnitude of God's love for us appears in John 3, verse 16 when Jesus said,

For God so loved the world, that he gave his only begotten Son, that whosoever believeth in him should not perish, but have everlasting life (KJV).

This was one of the first verses we committed to memory as a child, but our early familiarity with it perhaps overshadowed its true importance. For as powerful and perfect as God is, there is a part of Him which feels our needs, suffers our hurts and our losses. This is the God who gave not out of His plenty, but out of His only. This is the God who skimmed not off the top of His vast wealth for His people, but gave us His only Son. A gift always means more when the person giving it sacrifices either by time, money, or personal hardship. God gave us the best He had—His most prized possession. Then He watched, although not uncaring or powerless, as the inhabitants of the earth refused His Son, ridiculed, and finally killed Him. Shamefully the world reviled the Son of God, wrongfully accusing Him of crimes of which He was innocent, but God had a dream:

For God sent not his son into the world to condemn the world; but that the world through him might be saved (John 3:17, KJV).

And God also had love:

This is how God showed His love among us: He sent his one and only Son into the world that we might live through Him. This is love: not that we loved God, but that he loved us and sent his Son as an atoning sacrifice for our sins (I John 4:9, 10, NIV).

If you are striving for some purpose in your life, to attain a goal of great eminence, *this is it!* Jesus Chist is the *savior* of the world!

Jesus

The man Jesus was an exception from birth, half human, half spiritual. His mother was Mary, His father God. Jesus had been with God from the beginning. All things were made by Him. In Him was life. Grace and truth came into the world by Him (John 1).

We do not think of Jesus Christ as a human being, as a man with red blood running through His veins, sore muscles in His back, and chapped, rough hands. However, the humanity of Christ is what makes His teachings viable in our lives. It was His ability to reason, to feel, to perceive, to love, to hate, to be angry, and to feel pain as a human which lifts us above the toil and suffering of this world. If Jesus had not been able to experience the same feelings we experience, how could He possibly hope for our belief in his teachings when He said,

> Blessed are they which are persecuted for righteousness sake: for theirs is the kingdom of heaven (Matthew 5:10, KJV).

or,

> Therefore, take no thought, saying, What shall we eat? or, What shall we drink? or, Where withal shall we be clothed? (Matthew 6:31, KJV).

It is certainly easy for us to attribute Jesus' ability to withstand adversity to His spiritual powers. After all, He was the Son of God. We know Jesus lived a vagabond's existence upon the earth after He left Mary and Joseph's house.

> Foxes have holes, and birds of the air have nests; but the Son of man hath not where to lay his head (Luke 9:58, KJV).

The skeptic would say, "Jesus realized this was only a temporary situation with Him. He knew He would soon leave and dwell with God." But, unquestionably, the suffering of Jesus during His crucifixion, as recorded in the Gospels, should convince any skeptic of our Savior's desire to endure torturous, physical pain so that we might be saved. Other passages also attest to Jesus humanity.

When Peter, James, and John accompanied Him to Gethsemane, He began "to be sorrowful and troubled" (Matthew 26:37, KJV). Then He said to them, "My soul is overwhelmed with sorrow to the point of death. Stay here and keep watch with me" (Matthew 26:37,38, NIV). Jesus displayed the very human characteristic of wanting His friends near during a time of great difficulty.

Then Jesus left them, and going a little farther, fell with His face to the ground and prayed, "Oh my Father, if it be possible, let this cup pass from me: Nevertheless, not as I will, but as thou wilt" (Matthew 26:39, KJV). Another human trait. Jesus wanted to do His Father's will, but He didn't want to suffer in the process. How often have we felt the very same way?

Still more beautiful evidence of Jesus' humanity and His great love for His disciples, for us, and for His Father, is found in John 17. Let me urge you to read this prayer from the New International Version. It is here that these verses come alive, adding vivid imagery to the words spilling from Jesus's heart. He asks God to *protect* His followers from the evil one, just as He had *protected* them. This is the Jesus I want praying for me, interceding on my behalf before the throne of God.

> It is Christ that died, yea rather, that is risen again, who is even at the right hand of God, who also maketh intercession for us (Romans 8:34, KJV).

Only one who has suffered as we suffer can relate to our everyday problems, our ongoing battle against sin and its folly. Jesus endured that suffering so that we might have hope.

Freedom to Become Slaves (Romans 6:15-23, NIV)

One of the greatest privileges we have as American women is our freedom. Bloody wars have been waged on the battlefields of the world to insure our rights to life, liberty, and the pursuit of happiness. There are none of us who have ever experienced the tyranny of oppression from a dictatorial head of state. But when a woman lives in sin, she is a slave to sin, because we are slaves to the one we obey. If Satan has control of our heart, we are a slave to sin which leads to death.

Thanks to God we do not have to remain slaves to sin. Through our obedience to Jesus Christ, we have been set free from sin and have become slaves to righteousness.

But now that you have been set free from sin and have become slaves to God, the benefit you reap leads to holiness and the result is eternal life (v. 22).

Just as a woman submits herself to her husband by obedience, we must submit ourselves totally to Christ becoming a willful servant. We can not be coerced into slavery by fear, but rather we must gladly become slaves to do the will of our Master. The apostle Peter refers to himself as a "servant of Jesus Christ" in the book of second Peter. Jude, the youngest brother of Jesus, was also his servant.

Then how can a *slave* inherit eternal life?

But when the time had fully come, God sent his son, born of a woman, born under law, to redeem those under law, that we might receive the full rights of sons. Because you are sons, God sent the Spirit of his son into our hearts, the Spirit who calls out, Abba, Father. So you are no longer a slave, but a son: and since you are a son, God has made you also an heir (Galatians 4:4-7, NIV).
Note: See also Romans 8:12-17.

When we put to death the misdeeds or transgressions of our body, we will live and become God's children. If we are children, then we are heirs with Christ. If we share in His sufferings, so will we also share in His glory.

Now, Back to the List

Let's take a look at our lists for a moment. Does the name Jesus appear on yours? When I was first asked to make a list, it was during a very low period in my spiritual life. My list contained all the proper things. Is that why Jesus appeared on your list, because you thought it was the proper thing to do? God was at the top of my list, the church was also there. I was pretty pleased with it, until my counselor had looked it over and handed it back to me. At the very top of the page, he had written "Jesus." The name appeared nowhere else on the paper. I had forgotten the most important person in my life.

Since that dreadful day, the chief goal of my life has been concentrated on learning about Jesus, reading His words over and over again, giving them careful study, relating them to my own personal needs. With this study came the realization that I had never really known the man or His teachings. Sadly, most of us don't.

Jesus' Church

Misconceptions

Often it is hard for us to understand the wisdom of God, but the testing of our faith comes in the most peculiar ways. Take, for example, the church. When Jesus departed the earth, He left the foundation for His church. It was really a quite simple organization—a worldwide group of repentant believers who had declared their allegiance to Christ through the uncomplicated act of baptism. Each separate entity, or congregation, was to be overseen by shepherds, or elders. The main purpose of each group was two-fold—the nurturing and uplifting of each individual by the whole to gain strength against Satan, and the conversion of lost souls to the way of Christ.

Then man stepped in and the concept of simple Christianity became confused by divisions, power struggles, and the human inability to trust God. Today the church has become a displaced part of God's overall plan for salvation. Many members who have named Christ as the Son of God have forsaken the assembly of the church and also its work. A great number of the ones who are not happy in their local congregations complain about everything from plastic communion cups to the temperature of the building. They don't like the preacher and the other members aren't friendly enough.

We must make a distinction here and now about the difference between the church of our Lord and the congregations assembling on the earth. These two groups may very well differ on what is Christlike and what is not. This may be confusing to you at first, but think of it this way. Our allegiance is not to a denomination but to Jesus Christ.

Sadly for many Christians, the church is just another "social club" because Satan has prevented their knowledge of the true nature of the church. We become more concerned abour wearing our best to the worship than about giving our best to the Lord. We are more concerned about who's going to pay for the gas in the church bus than using that bus in some beneficial ministry. Members are leaving in droves, dropping out of the local work, but professing Christianity while at the same time committing spiritual adultery with the world (James 4:4). In the past few years, we have seen a resurgence in church growth among the fundamentalist groups where religion tends to be more heartfelt. This is primarily because these religious sects are appealing to the *basic* needs in a person's life.

It is safe to say that many congregations are in the death grips of men who would be "bosses" never giving a thought for the people of God or His will concerning the governing of a body of saints. The church is scarred with haughty men who wear their titles in a prideful manner. A minister once said that the greatest disappointments of his life came from fellow Christians, some leaders in the Lord's church. He expected persecution from the world, but not from his brothers in Christ.

See to it that no one takes you captive through hollow and deceptive philosophy, which depends on human tradition and the basic principles of this world rather than on Christ (Colossians 2:8, NIV).

So how can we avoid these disappointments and discouragements we face in the church?

The Church's Beauty

In the church we see more of God's beautiful network of spiritual authority. Just as He gave proper organization to the physical family, He also gave it to His spiritual family. Christ is the supreme head of the church (Colossians 1:18), with elders directing the affairs of the church (I Timothy 5:17) on earth. In I Corinthians 12, a lengthy list is given of the various works of individual Christians. This is the spiritual plan. If followed, it works.

Our love for Jesus is directly shown by our participation in His church and its work. After all, He sacrificed His blood to give it to us (Ephesians 5:25). Why are we hesitant to take full advantage of the blessings contained therein?

A local congregation of the church is probably only as strong as its leadership—its elders, deacons and ministers. There must be more teaching for men who desire to be shepherds and deacons. First, we must strictly adhere to the qualifications in Titus 1 and I Timothy 3 in selecting our leaders. When men and women attempt to amend God's standards, mediocre leadership is often the result. One of the greatest thrills in a Christian's life is to be associated with men who are indeed shepherds (I Peter 5:1-3, KJV) keeping close vigil over each little lamb in the flock. It gives one a feeling of security to know that God's plan is working through His devoted servants.

However, we may come to the point in time when our spiritual leaders cease to lead. If this happens in our own congregation, we must carry on Jesus' work regardless of what others are doing. Herein lies the beauty of Christ's church. We are all one, but at the same time separate. If the leaders of your congregation are no longer progressive and energetic, if they have lain down on the job, you do not have to form a committee to perform a good deed.

One of the greatest frustrations we face as women is the apparent lack of sensitivity by some leaders to the problems facing our congregations. Often the attitude is taken that if a problem is swept under the rug, it will eventually go away. The reason I mention this now is that over and over again in my conversations with other women, this same demon keeps rearing its head. Some of this could be attributed to sour grapes, but to dismiss it entirely on those grounds would be unkind to devout Christian women everywhere living with this problem. As a person without authority in the spiritual network, the feeling of helplessness is almost overwhelming for some and has caused them to become embittered and hardened toward the church.

If you are faced with a depressing situation of non-growth in your own congregation, stop fretting and complaining about it. Get up and get to work for Jesus. Even if others are not doing God's will, your genuine desire to serve might be contagious. Other women may well wish to join your efforts for the Lord. You can work out of your home taking on any challenge in the name of Christ. It only takes one Christian to make a difference. Remember your allegiance is to Jesus Christ and to no one else.

Chapter Seven

1. Discuss Jesus' origin and his place within the Trinity.
2. What type of personality do you think Nicodemus had? Why was his interest in Jesus so important to us?
3. Why has it been so difficult for the people of the world to accept Jesus as the Son of God?

4. Reflect upon the freedoms we have in Christ. Can we have these freedoms no matter where we live, work, etc?
5. Does our Father recognize you as one of his church members? What are you doing to perpetuate the work of the church?

CHAPTER 8

Single And Single Again

The Single Woman

A woman instinctively prepares herself for marriage. From an early age, she learns mothering skills from her own mother. Sometime later, usually by the mid-twenties, most young women desire to be married.

It is with great expectation that we dream of a home with a husband and children. But for many women, marriage never comes. Some singles are most happy with this arrangement, while others are miserable. Some are content being single, and far prefer this lifestyle. Others just want to be married.

In observing most women who never marry, the conclusion is that it has little to do with personality, physical looks, or ability. Unmarried women are, more often than not, bright, energetic, and very self-reliant. Today, there are more college graduates among our singles. Highly-educated women are bringing a wealth of knowledge and expertise to the Lord's work.

The single woman has one distinct, clear-cut advantage over her married counterpart. Unencumbered, she must answer only to God for all her actions since she is not involved in a marriage situation and not the mother of several children. She basically is free to live out her days on earth as a being totally bound to God and to Him alone. The apostle Paul speaks of this in I Corinthians 7:34.

> The unmarried woman careth for the things of the Lord, that she may be holy both in body and in spirit: but she that is married

careth for the things of the world, how she may please her husband (KJV).

There is a certain stabilty to be found in marriage and also in sexual fulfillment. The desire for these is proper, but if you are single, make the most of your other opportunities. Someday you might marry, but until then decide that "this is my life, God gave it to me, and I'm going to make the very best of it I can." Don't waste precious time wishing your life were some other way. This is a good rule for any Christian woman to follow.

Being Single Again

To be truly happy in the eyes of the traditional world, a woman must find her prince charming, ride off into the sunset with him on a blazing stallion, and live happily ever after. Wouldn't it be nice if life were really that way?

However, we know that rainbows don't last, and that our idea of "happily ever after" can come crashing down around us at any time. If this section does not reflect the state of your marriage at present (and for very obvious reasons I hope it doesn't), you probably know of someone—perhaps a dear friend or a relative—who has had to endure the trauma of divorce, the agony over the loss of a mate by death, plus the responsibility of raising children alone. None of us know when we might be hastily cast into this same category ourselves.

The Dreadful D's—Divorce & Death

The Divorced Woman

Marriage can be blissful. It gives us an opportunity to develop a relationship which can last a lifetime. We can love and share with one individual all the deep thoughts of our heart. But if the love goes away and trust is lost, bitterness and resentment quickly creep in to fill the void.

For years we avoided the word *divorce* like the plague. If

we ignored it, maybe it would go away. Every year approximately two out of four marriages fail in America and more of these failures are occuring among Christians than ever before. In the Lord's church, we can no longer ignore the fact that Christian women are suffering from broken marriages just as the women in the world are suffering.

As we learned before, God hates divorce (Malachi 2:16), but he does not hate the divorced person. There are some circumstances, not including adultery, to which Paul seems to refer in I Corinthians 7 when a man and woman will separate.

> And unto the married I command, yet not I, but the Lord, Let not the wife depart from her husband: But and if she depart, let her remain unmarried, or be reconciled to her husband: and let not the husband put away his wife (I Corinthians 7:10,11, KJV).

The King James Version uses the word "depart" in this passage while the New International says "separate." The Greek word is *charidzo* which is the same word used by Jesus in Matthew 19:9 when he refers to divorce. There is no concept of "legal separation" in the New Testament. The wife could separate from her husband or be divorced from him, but she was to remain unmarried.

What would prompt a woman to leave her husband and seek a divorce for any reason other than infidelity? Alcoholism, abusive beatings, and refusal by the husband to provide a living are just a few of the problems forcing women to flee their homes seeking refuge for themselves and their children. Personally, if my husband beat me once a week, one day my children and I would privately slip away never to be heard from again. It would be very difficult to live in the same house with him fearing for my life and perhaps also for the lives of my children. I can think of two separate instances that I know of personally where Christian men have waited for their wives to return home while they toyed with loaded guns. Each man eventually took his own life. One wife escaped from her home and the other hesitated to return to her home fearing for her life. Violence is a real threat even in some Christian marriages.

The point I am trying to make is that we cannot possibly know what goes on behind the doors of a private dwelling. Therefore, we should not judge. If a woman comes to us and is divorced, we should encourage her to live for the Lord, not condemn her marital status (Romans 14:13).

It is a fact that *normal* people (i.e. those married) don't quite know what to do with divorced people. We want to know why the marriage failed. Some of us even think it is our right to know. What could the divorced woman have done to avoid the divorce? As human beings we are not always kind in our investigation of the matter and don't always consider the fact that a wife (or husband) might be totally innocent of any fault in the break-up of the marriage contract.

Once a remark was made about a very dear friend of mine who happened to be divorced and had returned to her hometown with her children.

"She is so spoiled," a lady said, as if that were the reason her marriage failed. In all the time I knew this woman, she displayed only the very best Christian behavior and attitudes. This kind of irreverent, loose talk can do nothing in helping a divorced person recover from what must be a dreadful, painful situation.

Our benevolence toward those in the church who have had to suffer the humiliation and embarrassment of the dissolution of their marriage is of utmost importance. Our love and support may be just what the divorced person needs to go on and live a full and prosperous life for God. We should never be guilty of prying into a divorced person's private life, but rather we should instruct them in what the Lord wants all of us to do to be right in His sight. Remember, it is ultimately up to the individual to make her own choice about divorce and remarriage. In the final analysis, she will be responsible for her actions.

The Widowed Woman

One of the most difficult things in the world for a woman to do is to make the sad journey to a bleak cemetery on a cold, rainy day and place a coffin containing the body of her husband in the ground. First comes the numbness of shock. She must be dreaming. She'll wake up, and her husband will still be asleep next to her. Everything is really alright. Then the reality sets in. The man she loves is gone. She is alone.

As women, we are faced with the probability of outliving our husbands. After the marriage ceremony, we never thought about being single again. All of our friends are married, all the fun things are done by couples. Suddenly a widow doesn't quiet fit in. Once she did when she was married and the kids were still home, but not now. She is caught in the "fifth-wheel" syndrome.

In studying the book of Ruth, we usually pass rather hurriedly over the first fifteen verses of the book to get to Ruth's beautiful speech of compassion. Sometime before that, however, we should look at the agony Naomi must have experienced after first losing her husband and then, her two sons. How would you feel if you had to bury three members of your immediate family right now? And to make it worse, Naomi was living in a foreign country with two pagan daughters-in-law. But she was a woman of personal determination possessed with a trust in God. As you remember the story, her life became full and happy again after the birth of her grandson Obed.

Surely Naomi experienced the pangs of sorrow felt by every other widow. It is very easy to sit around and feel sorry for yourself, to stay indoors and not desire to be around others. This may be most difficult for the older woman who resists change. This behavior, however, is natural and can be expected for some time after the initial loss of any loved one. But sooner or later, the fact has to be faced: you must carry on. But you are not alone. *God is with you!* Of course bad things happen to good people, and as sure as we are born, we will die. The better able we are to accept this part of our physical life—the inevitability of death—the better we can manage when it does come.

While a widow, *fill your life with love.* There are so many things to be done to show our love for God and our fellow man. So many are dying in sin, never having heard the simple message of Jesus Christ. You may be just the one to tell them. There are sick to be visited and assisted, elderly who need care and attention, and there are always children who need to be taught both in the Bible class and in the public schools where there are usually excellent volunteer programs available. Just keep busy and in so doing you'll find something that's right for you.

One of the best reasons for a widow to keep busy is to stay out of trouble. If we are not occupied, we tend to talk too much and too often. Some widows never remarry after their husbands' deaths, choosing instead to devote their lives to the church and doing the Lord's work. This leaves no time nor inclination on their part to engage in gossip or idleness against which Paul warns so sternly in I Timothy 5:13.

> And withal they learn to be idle, wandering about from house to house: and not only idle, but tattlers also and busy-bodies, speaking things which they ought not (KJV).

A Christian widow need not be like these women, but should display hospitality, "devoting herself to all kinds of good deeds" (I Timothy 5:9,10, NIV).

Common Problems and Common Goals

The single woman encounters certain common problems and goals whether she be unmarried, divorced, or widowed. It is staggering to realize that a woman who has been married, possibly all of her adult life, can suddenly, either by divorce or death, find herself in the same single boat with a woman who has never been married. It is here that the single woman must possess an abundant faith in God and self-confidence in her own abilities if she is to survive. For the woman who has never married, these problems and goals are a normal succession of life's patterns. But for the divorced or widowed woman, the sudden plunge into an unexpected lifestyle can be overwhelming.

The following areas are where these women must excel.

1. The single woman must take responsibility for her own life. Married women have their husbands to lean on, but a single woman has to be independent and rely upon her own best judgments. In a rather mysterious way, this is one of the most challenging parts of single life. But she must be careful from whom she takes advice, heeding only that which is based on the principles Jesus taught. There are those, some quite innocently, who would try to run her life, but she must not let them. She must practice being independent and learn to trust in God.

2. The single woman must support herself.

According to Jesus' teachings in Matthew 5,6, and 7, this is not an area where a single should waste valuable time worrying. Fear causes worry, so to reduce the anxiety over the future, one should prepare for it. Get a good education. For the divorced woman and the widow, there are plenty of jobs to be had even if you have never before received a paycheck. The jobs available may include hard manual labor, and the pay may be less than desirable, but dive in and gain some experience. Others will notice your determination. Pray to your Father in heaven and He will provide the strength you need.

Remember before, when we mentioned that if something appears twice in God's word, its wise to take a second look? In Matthew 6:8 and 32, we are told that our heavenly Father knows our need even *before* we ask Him. Isn't that comforting? God will sustain us if we rely upon Him. He only wants us to ask.

3. The single woman must contend with being alone.

One of the most miserable weeks of my life occured just after my sophomore year of college. I had moved off campus into a small apartment with two other girls. My wedding was only three short months away. In the bright sunlight of early summer, everything suddenly turned gray. The two roommates left on vacation and my fiancé went out of town on a business trip. The campus was deserted, I had no car, I was starting a new job, and the city felt cold and fearful. I was so lonely.

However, just because a person is alone it doesn't follow that she has to be lonely. Loneliness is a state of the mind and can be conquered by positive steps.

First, take care of your body. Exercise and eat properly. (Try not to overeat or undereat.) Be good to yourself. Set up little rituals of pleasant pursuits—a long, hot soak in the tub, a new record of soothing music, or lunch with a friend. Be active. Be involved.

Second, reach out to other people. The loneliest person in the world is the one who cares only for herself. The concept of "me, my, mine and I" is foreign to Jesus' teachings. He was a solitary figure—a single. But through His goodness He helped others overcome their burdens. In the same way, single women can administer to the needs of others.

4. The single is to be sexually and morally pure.

We live in a time when the sexual revolution is rampant among singles as well as marrieds. Bars are everywhere, even in the better restaurants. From every direction—on television, in the movies, in magazines, etc.—sexual overtones come to bear on everything we see and hear. The single Christian knows and believes that fornication and adultery are wrong, but it is what is expected and accepted by many of her peers.

Jesus Christ was the ultimate single, and was no doubt *tempted* by sexual desires (Hebrews 4:15). Remember, He was a man! But He was without sin (I Peter 2:22). It is through the grace of God that a single can resist temptation.

For the grace of God that brings salvation has appeared to all men, It teaches us to say "No" to ungodliness and worldly passions, and to live self-controlled, upright and godly lives in this present age, while we wait for the blessed hope—the glorious appearing of our great God and Savior, Jesus Christ, who gave himself for us to redeem us from all wickedness and to purify for himself a people that are his very own, eager to do what is good (Titus 2:11-14, NIV).

Often it is easier for an unmarried woman to abide by this teaching simply from a biological standpoint, a virgin having never known the intimacy of marriage. Therefore, the divorced woman and the widow must take extra care to guard themselves from Satan's ability to play upon this specific need in their lives.

Marriage and Remarriage

The commission of a marriage for the single woman can bring great joy to her life. Careful selection of a mate is imperative if the union has any real chance of longevity and happiness. Avoid rushing into a marriage to erase the singleness of your life. It is far better to be single wishing to be married, than married wishing to be single. There are much worse things in one's life than not being married, and one worse thing is being married to the wrong person. Due to the spiraling divorce rate, many ministers now require the prospective bride and groom's participation in a marriage preparatory seminar for a period of six weeks prior to the nuptials. Also to be gravely considered is the spiritual devotion of the man you plan to marry. Christians should marry only other Christians (2 Corinthians 6:14, NIV) thus strengthening the chances of a successful marriage.

If you are a widow considering remarriage, you must be very careful about your prospective husband. The second marriage can be just as wonderful and enduring as the first with proper preparation. Is the new man in your life—to one you have chosen to marry—devoted to Jesus Christ? If he isn't, then how is he going to help you with your spiritual life? It would be better for you to remain unmarried than to live with someone who might interfere with your dedication to the Father.

If you find yourself single again after divorce, please consider the following things. Do you have a right to remarry? If there is any doubt on your part after careful and thorough study of God's word, then you should remain unmarried for the remainder of your life. This is not a pleasant and easy task to consider, but it is the safest.

If you feel you have a scriptural right to remarry, please consider carefully the person you have chosen. Too often divorced women find that the only men available for marriage in their age bracket are themselves divorced with an ex-wife and children to complicate the triangle. This can especially be a problem if the man is a Christian and his ex-wife is not. She can make his life a virtual torment on earth. You must also consider whether a divorced man has a scriptural reason for his divorce, and if he is indeed free to marry again. As you see, the problems can continue to mount up if two divorced people are considering marriage to each other.

In any remarriage involving a divorced woman, remember that if a child of God is to be pleasing to God, she may not be able to do whatever makes her happy. This is why the Christian must be objective and *always* put God first. If you do this, there will be no doubts.

The Children

Children are a blessing, but in times of divorce or the death of their father, they rapidly become victims. According to the Bureau of Labor Statistics there are now 6,147,000 American homes composed of a woman, at least one child, and no man. Also, 4,162,000 of these women are working outside the home (March, 1982).

Children undoubtedly suffer when their parents cannot get along or when death comes. Often they are uprooted from their homes and schools and separated from friends and classmates. There is the vital need to quickly establish a settled environment for them—a home filled with love provided by a mother who is supported by the love of God. Get your children into Bible class and give them the foundation of faith in Jesus Christ. You'll soon see the difference in their lives. If any problem arises which you are not capable of handling, seek help either from a Christian friend, a minister, an elder, or a social agency.

There is a wealth of knowledge of good which flows between Christian women. There is risk in loving and reaching out to others for the single as well as the married. But it has always been God's plan for His children to support one another. Whether married or single, we all need to rally around each other offering encouragement to the lonely and troubled. The single woman has a very important and distinct position in the Lord's church. She can help others accept and enjoy the many different facets of single life.

Chapter Eight

1. What are the positive aspects of being single? The negative?
2. Make a list of ways in which a single woman can serve the Lord more effectively than a married woman. Do you believe this is a possibility?
3. As a married woman, do you find yourself prejudiced against single women, especially those who are divorced? If so, why?
4. As a Christian, are you equipped to give proper advice about remarriage to one who is divorced? Is your counsel based upon scripture?

CHAPTER 9

Overweight and Out Of Shape

Don't You Dare Skip This Chapter!

Have you ever wondered what this topic has to do with spirituality? Does a Christian really have a right to be overweight and out of shape? (I know. Now I've gone to meddling!)

I've been pudgy for the last fifteen years. My teenage daughter once said to me, "I've never seen you skinny." That statement really made me feel sad because it was true. I had lost my self-control where food was concerned and was definitely lacking in any athletic prowess. Walking up a flight of stairs left me breathless. And there was no physical reason to be in the shape I was in, except neglect.

Even though we are in the middle of a physical fitness boom, most women, especially mothers, find they are actually too busy to take care of their bodies. Yet research has taught us that there is a definite link between how our physical bodies feel and how we think. Advertisements may say, "Fat is beautiful," but don't you believe it. Obesity causes low self-esteem. The strategists of Madison Avenue look for beautiful, *thin* people to sell their products. The tailored, well-designed clothes on the market are made for women with small figures. Fat is not beautiful. It is *harmful!*

If you're a bit rotund and happen to be reading this in the company of others, don't be embarrassed. They all know you're a little overweight. After all, it's a hard thing to hide. There may be a lot of excuses for the size you're in, but none of them are good enough. Only 2% (approximately) of the overweight people in America are obese because of illness. The rest of us are just out of control. Let's face it, girls. Some of us have gone to pot!

A dear friend has been very obese since childhood. He doesn't want to be, but he is. He is also a minister. At a church where he applied for a job, one of the few complaints registered against him was from a couple who were concerned about his weight. They reasoned that the teenagers of the congregation might not listen to him if he taught against drugs or immorality, because in looking at him they could clearly see a person who lacked self-control at least in regard to food. These parents had a good point. If one lacks self-control, how can he talk to a person who is outside of Christ about being controlled by Him? It is not an impossibility, but it does make the task more difficult.

Just how far can a Christian woman go before she becomes a glutton? Even if we don't like to admit it, gluttony is an indiscretion, if not a sin (Luke 7:34, KJV).

Now for all you others, even the "five-foot-two, eyes of blue, 105-pounders", your problem may not be your weight, but it may be your shape. Could you, right now, run a mile without stopping? Could you even walk a mile without stopping? Would the least bit of physical exertion put you in danger of cardiac arrest? And if you're trying to tell me that all that housework you do, all those carpools, running here and there to meet a schedule, are exercise enough, forget it. That's not exercise. That's exhaustion! In order for exercise to help tone up your muscles, heart and lungs, a person must participate in some sort of sustained activity for twenty to thirty minutes, at least three to four times a week—minimum. Even though a woman is slim, it does not necessarily follow that she is in good shape.

Now to the very heart of this matter. Our bodies are the temple of the Holy Spirit of God.

What? know ye not that your body is the temple of the Holy Ghost which is in you, which ye have of God, and ye are not your own? For ye are bought with a price: Therefore glorify God in your body, and in your Spirit, which are God's (I Corinthians 6:19,20, KJV).

Have you really stopped to comprehend what that says to you and me as Christians. The Scriptures tell us that the Holy Spirit is very important to God and that He treasures it highly.

Wherefore I say unto you, All manner of sin and blasphemy shall be forgiven unto men: but the blasphemy against the Holy Ghost shall not be forgiven unto men (Matthew 12:31, KJV).

Bearing these facts in mind, don't you think that the Holy Spirit of God deserves a decent, unpolluted place in which to dwell? As Christians we have the obligation, yea even the privilege, of being the best we can for the Lord. Remember, He doesn't want second best.

Taking Care of Your Body

The women of America are among the best educated, most accomplished females in the universe, but on occasion we don't use our intelligence Often rushed, we eat whatever is convenient, hardly caring about caloric or nutritional content. We're on a roller coaster riding the waves of prosperity. It's time to slow down and start planning our lives. It's time to get *smart!*

In taking proper care of the body, there are four main areas in which to concentrate our efforts:

1. Nutrition—The basis of any good health is good nutrition. Start with fresh fruits and vegetables and lean meats. Avoid white sugar and drugs such as caffeine and nicotine. Once, I went on a very strict diet to combat a medical problem, and on the third day suffered a most severe headache due to caffeine withdrawal. My body was revolting in a harsh way to deprivation of something it had come to depend upon

for survival. The body actually takes on a lighter feeling when one completely leaves off sugar and sweets. Those who fast report that it takes about three days for the body to rid itself of all impurities. Then they're suddenly endowed with an incredible ability to think more clearly.

2. Exercise—"One, two, three, four. . . ." (Oh, how I hate those words.) The best all around exercise for everyone is walking. Nearly everyone can participate without suffering any adverse affects. Start by walking ten minutes a day, five days a week, and gradually build up to thirty minutes a day. Walk in the morning or late evening when it's cool and walk rapidly. If you get bored going by yourself, drag the dog or a kid along.
3. Pap smear—Women habitually neglect this one simple little task. Oh, it's the pits to have a physical, but once a year is no big thing. Just think, you might actually save your life and be around to see your grandchildren. This simple routine test has saved many lives and should be a serious part of our overall health care.
4. Obesity—Medically, obesity begins when a person is twenty-five pounds over their ideal body weight. Physical problems such as edema, hypertension, and diabetes are sometimes brought on or complicated by excessive weight. And there are also emotional problems. If you're in this category of being overweight, it would be wise to see your family doctor for a complete physical. Then decide what kind of food plan you want to begin to lose the weight you need to lose. *(No crash diets!)* Then pray. God will help you accomplish your goal. Don't restrict His ability to see you through this phase of your life. With the loss of weight and proper exercise, you'll look better, feel better, and probably prolong your life.

Taking Responsibility for Yourself

A person may not want to admit it, but one is fat only because one chooses to be. You manage your time or time manages you. You handle money or money handles you. You control your eating or your eating controls you. "But I can't help myself," some protest. Our lives are in our own hands. Resist Satan and he will flee from you (James 4:7). We are responsible for ourselves. When we begin to take responsibility for our own lives, we will begin to feel better.

Self-Control

The Christian woman really has no excuse to be out of control. Why are alcoholics addicted to drink? Because it controls them. What happens if a diabetic refuses to strictly adhere to a special diet and take medication properly? He or she could possibly face coma, amputation of a limb, or blindness. Confronted with a life or death ultimatum, we usually summon the courage necessary to follow a program that will make us feel and look better. Why then wait until weight becomes so extreme that it endangers the heart and other vital organs by causing too much strain on them? This thing of being on a diet day in and day out gets old and discouraging. A Christian woman has the ability to take charge of her life and point herself in a direction that is both beneficial and sane.

The apostle Paul said, "I can do all things through Christ which strengtheneth me" (Phillipians 4:13, KJV). We can do the same. If you read only that one verse over and over every day for a week, you'll find a new sense of direction, hope, and zeal invading your mind. Where you were once overcome by an impulse to eat, you'll now have the strength and will power to suppress it.

A friend had lost over one hundred pounds following stomach stapling surgery. She had reached a point in her life where the doctor had told her she would die if she didn't lose weight. She was so addicted to a certain brand of soda pop that every night before turning in, she placed one can of her favorite beverage in the refrigerator to drink at breakfast the next morning. (The drink had to be in a can, not in a bottle.) One evening she discovered that her son had drunk the last can of pop, and she went to bed knowing she wouldn't have a drink in the morning. After tossing and turning for awhile, she arose around 2:30 A.M., went to a nearby all-night convenience store, bought one can of pop, brought it home, placed it in the refrigerator, went to bed and slept the rest of the night. It seems preposterous, but if you must have that cup of coffee every morning, or a pill, or a cigarette to get going, you also recognize the signs of addiction.

Like a city whose walls are broken down is a man who lacks self-control (Proverbs 25:28, NIV).

The best way to be in control is to resist temptation. And the best way to do that is by fleeing from it. Whatever your temptation might be, put it away. Get rid of it. And always remember, it's a daily battle. Day, by day, by day.

Practice Self-Esteem

I hate to make a mistake worse than anyone on the face of this earth. If I'm not careful, I'll carry around the guilt that inevitably comes with mistakes. I didn't even know what self-esteem was until I became an adult, but now I know what it is, and it's a treasure we should protect for our own best interest.

Jesus is the great physician who entreats us to cast all of our anxieties upon Him.

Come unto me, all ye that labor and are heavy laden, and I will give you rest. Take my yoke upon you, and learn of me: for I am meek and lowly in heart: and ye shall find rest unto your souls (Matthew 11:28,29, KJV).

Not one put down there, but yet, in our lives we are assaulted on every front—at work, at home and sometimes even in the house of worship—by those who seem only to want to belittle and discourage. If one is not mature emotionally, she can slip into the realm of low self-esteem. Don't let it happen. *You are a wonderful person capable of doing many different things well.* Repeat this statement over and over to yourself. Believe it!

Protect Your Time

There is a thief among us. He sneaks in unawares stealthily, insidiously robbing us blind. He steals our *time.*

Loss of time occurs in one of two ways—through procrastination, and through lack of maintanance. It's easy to put things off, day after day, until we are faced with a mountain of unclean laundry, dirty bathrooms, and overgrown lawns. At work, the desk piles deeper and deeper in unresolved paperwork. We feel pressed by common, everyday jobs that have to be done no matter how long we put them off.

Learn to work efficiently and well, making lists and notes if you must. Guard each valuable moment by putting your best into the task at hand. (If you stay home and feel you never accomplish anything, *turn off the TV set!*) Don't be guilty of procrastinating.

If our time is used wisely, we can avoid habitual rushing. Watch yourself on a typical Tuesday. See how often you find yourself rushing about, first to school, then to the grocery, even to the mailbox. It's hurry, hurry, hurry. Why? Are we afraid dinner might be half an hour late? So what? You might even miss two minutes of your favorite television show. Who'll know the difference two years from now—or even two days? *Learn to slow down!*

Conclusion

As mothers, we try so hard to see that our children are properly fed. We take them to the doctor if they don't respond to an aspirin. If hubby has one little touch of indigestion, we're afraid he might be suffering a heart attack. But when it comes to ourselves, we generally put off our good health for the sake of our family, even to the point of skipping dental and medical appointments. *We are very valuable to our families and their development.* We must not neglect our bodies, either physically or spiritually.

In the New Testament, we are encouraged to support and help one another (I John 4:11). If you can't afford to be in a professional weight-loss group, one could be formed from members of your own Bible class. You could meet once a week, weigh-in, and encourage each other in your individual weight-loss program. There is no real magic to losing weight. Just eat less and exercise more.

We all have an interest in seeing that our bodies are in their best shape. If we're sound physically, it can help us be sound mentally. A strong mental determination is what makes a Christian a dynamic force for Jesus Christ. If we can develop a well-equipped physical companion for our minds, our dedication to God will take on a new focus. We will be able to boldly declare our love for God and His Son to those about us.

Chapter Nine

1. List the ways in which we neglect our physical health. Are you guilty of neglecting your body?
2. Discuss the relationship between our physical health and our mental health.
3. How is our spiritual well-being influenced by the self-control we practice in our lives?
4. In what areas are we responsible for ourselves?

Chapter 10

Blue Mondays

Mondays are difficult days at best and sometimes every day seems like Monday. Dad, and often Mom, rolls out of bed early going back to the office to earn a few more dollars, while the kids head back to school. Mondays are dreaded by most of us, but "blue Mondays" really started a long time ago—probably in the era of our grandmothers. Back then, Monday was always washday. *Always!* The bluing substance added to the wash water to whiten the clothes became associated with the drudgery that nearly every woman faced every single Monday morning of her life. In my earliest recollection, my own grandmother had two large washtubs with a ringer mounted on top of one through which clean, wet clothes were pressed squeezing out the excess water. (For those of you too young to remember, this was the original "spin cycle".) It literally took all day to wash and then dry the clothes on a line. Of course, the day was a disaster if it rained or turned winter. The whole ordeal was enough to make anyone feel down and depressed. Unfortunately for us, our new, more modern washing machines haven't made the blues go away.

The Blahs

Everyone has a bad day now and then. The baby cries all night for no apparent reason, the water heater blows up soaking half the carpet down the hallway, or perhaps the hairdresser cuts a tad too much off your hair. These minor, or major if they're costly, irritations can drive a person up the wall, until you feel like running and screaming through the streets. Your best friend doesn't even care about your problems because her teenage son just got a ticket for speeding and has to appear in court. Call it what you may—the blues or the blahs—but this nagging agitation can get you down if you let it. Sometimes we feel low simply from boredom, the sameness in our routine being the major culprit. Generally, however, our mood swing will last only a few hours or days, and a little diverse activity or excitement—even a good night's sleep—will quickly bring us back to our normal selves.

When we don't snap back quickly from the little ups and downs of life, we may have reached a state of depression. Tons of books have been written on the topic of depression and for every idea expressed by one learned expert on the subject, you'll most certainly find another qualified person who will disagree with that statement. Some of the books are okay, and some can only be understood if you have a degree in psychology. Here we are only interested in dealing with the very basic aspects of depression, hopefully in terms easily understood by the lay person.

Levels of Depression

The mind is a marvelous machine—a computer bank of stored material, instantly recalling important facts on a moment's notice. But the mind sometimes becomes bogged down, getting depressed, for reasons unknown to man. In the medical community, there are several theories and much speculation concerning the causes of depression, but no clear-cut reason has been found. And we are not immune to depressive thoughts merely because we are Christians.

There are varying levels of depression. Most are mild and are a normal outlet—a proper response to loss or stress. These degrees of depression can be brought on by grief, the loss of a job, or the loss of a girlfriend or boyfriend. It is perfectly natural and healthy to feel depressed under these circumstances. As your emotions are taxed, depression rises to dull them. This is a very appropriate reaction when facing the death of a loved one or some other great tragedy. Your mind actually gives your whole self a chance to accept what has happened and allows you a proper amount of time in which to adjust and be in control of your feelings.

Depression can also follow an illness or trauma. Several years ago, my mother barely survived a severe truck crash. She was confined to the hospital for seventeen days over the Christmas holidays with a full leg cast and months of tedious therapy ahead. Her spirits had been very high throughout the whole ordeal constantly reassuring the family she was alright. Her recovery proceeded very well until one day when my father and I were away from the house.

My sister was staying with our mother, and suddenly, without warning, Mother became very depressed and hysterical. A neighbor was summoned and called for an ambulance. When my mother reached the hospital emergency room, she was already regaining her composure and was well enough to return home. Her body and mind had simply suffered too much stress and pain over a prolonged period of time. After this episode of depression had passed, she continued to mend and completely recovered.

Post-partum depression is experienced by some women after the birth of a child. There is some tiredness and depression which naturally occurs following delivery. This is normal and usually lasts for only a few days or a couple of weeks. However, in some cases it can be prolonged.

Being plagued by quilt is also another major source of depression. Other sources are loneliness, the desire for material wealth, and an excessive competitive hostility—always needing to achieve, compulsively having to be the best.

A person can become depressed and stay depressed. Nothing really brings it on. It's just there like a dark, brooding cloud hanging over one's head. When this happens, the following four things are often experienced:

1—Sad thoughts. This is often characterized by the loss of one's smile.
2—The desire to sleep all the time. The person loses all interests in taking care of personal appearance (brushing of teeth, combing of hair, bathing, etc.).
3—Thoughts of suicide.
4—Unnatural fears.

When depression reaches any one of these levels and continues for more than three weeks, professional counseling becomes necessary. No amount of happy thoughts, exercise, or good diet will cause this type of depression to fade. This person needs professional help, either in the form of medication or counseling. It would be wise to consult a medical doctor for treatment.

Solutions for Depression

The whole spectrum of life free from depression must encompass our mental, spiritual and physical systems. If any one area is neglected, the body is deprived of a natural built in defense against anxieties and insecurities.

As hopeless as mild depression may seem at times, there are many available solutions to combat its effects. Our mind and our will can combine creating a terrific force bringing our emotions into submission with the rest of our body. Let's look at a few of the ways we can defeat depression.

1—Proper Thought Life

"For as he thinketh in his heart, so is he" (Proverbs 23:7, KJV). We are what we think, so a bad thought life is sure to make us feel depressed. My husband tells the story of how some of his college classmates had agreed among themselves to tell another classmate how badly he looked to see what affect, if any, it would have upon him. At breakfast one day, the young man felt perfectly alright, but during the day as he saw his friends one by one, they asked him if he felt sick. He began to feel poorly and by mid-day had retreated to his dorm and taken to his bed, too ill to move. Although a cruel joke, this deed clearly illustrates how our minds can play tricks on us, deceiving us into thinking something which is not true. The ultimate challenge to the Christian for a healthy, happy thought life is recorded in Phillipians 4:8

Finally, brethern, whatsoever things are true, whatsoever things are honest, whatsoever things are just, whatsoever things are pure, whatsoever things are lovely, whatsoever things are of good report; if there be any virtue, and if there be any praise, think on these things (KJV).

The simplistic beauty of the words honesty, justice, and praise seem to encase the soul with calm and add stability to our lives.

2—Conquer Loneliness

Due to the social aspect of our nature, almost everyone hates to be alone. But few of us are actually without friends. Even those who have fairly obnoxious personalities have some close friends. However, loneliness can occur even in a crowded room.

The prophet Elijah thought he was alone. After suffering one crisis after another, he was physically and emotionally drained. He had the worse case of the "juniper tree blues", and in I Kings 19:5, he asked God to just let him die. He figured he was the only person left on the face of the earth who trusted in God. But the Lord surprised him.

Yet I have left me seven thousand in Israel, all the knees of which have not bowed unto Baal, and every mouth which hath not kissed him (KJV).

There were still thousands of the Lord's servants active in His work that Elijah didn't even know. No matter how lonely we feel, we are seldom really alone. The Lord is always with us, keeping His promise: "I will never leave thee, nor forsake thee" (Hebrews 13:5, KJV).

A woman had moved into our city and felt totally overwhelmed by loneliness. An acquaintance was constantly being invited to one party after another, while this woman and her husband sat home, rarely enjoying any social activities. For six months the woman cried. She was angry and hurt that she had ever moved to such an unfriendly town. Then she hit upon a wonderful idea. If people wouldn't invite her into their homes, she would host her own parties. Suddenly, she had many new friends with common goals and Christian ideals, each happily visiting in her home seeking friendship. In turn, this couple was invited to other homes.

If you're lonely, reach out to others. Don't be interested only in yourself or your own desires. Make your life one of service. You'll find your life so crowded with new friends, you won't have time to be lonely.

3—Learn Contentment

The world is not big enough to satisfy our needs.

> Remove far from me vanity and lies: give me neither poverty nor riches; feed me with food convenient for me: Lest I be full, and deny thee and say, Who is the Lord? or lest I be poor, and steal, and take the name of my God in vain (Proverbs 30:8,9, KJV).

The New International Version says it a little plainer:

> Keep falsehood and lies far from me; give me neither poverty nor riches, but give me only my daily bread. Otherwise, I may have too much and disown you and say, "Who is the Lord?"

Learning to be content with what we have is one of the hardest lessons to learn. If we strive for what others have and never consider our Lord's wishes, we're only setting ourselves up for a fall. "Godliness with contentment is great gain" (I Timothy 6:6, KJV). Oh, that we would become wise and accept this biblical principle.

4—Avoid Negative People

It is our tendency to imitate those around us, so stay away from negative, bitter people. Most tend to be hateful and nasty once their inner selves are revealed. Instead, take negative thoughts and turn them into positive thoughts to build your character and make you a better person. Don't be sucked into a pool of slime by those who do not wish to better themselves. Leave them to their own negativism.

5—Build a Security Network

The feeling of being safe is very comforting. I remember as a child never worrying about bills, or death, or illness. But somewhere along the way to adulthood, anxieties mount over little things and can soon consume our whole outlook on life. Real, true security comes from our family and friends, our children, and our faith in the Lord. These "security blankets" cannot be bought with silver and gold. You should dwell upon places or things which make you feel happy—a magnificent view, a path winding through the woods, sitting in your favorite chair wrapped in a soft, old blanket with a cup of tea. Even the apostle Paul had the things he loved. He instructed the young minister, Timothy, in II Timothy 4:13 to bring his cloke to him, along with his books and parchments. Having the things around us which make us feel secure produces a warm, inner peace.

6—Maintain Balance

In many ways, we have lost our common sense. The world is rushing. We'd better get in step if we don't want to be left behind. Maintaining any kind of sanity in today's forum is almost a miracle. *Balance* is the key to good mental health. Keep physically fit by exercising your body. Eat well and get proper rest and sleep.

The Scottish veternarian, James Herriott, wrote about a sheep he once saw who was near death after the birth of a lamb. He felt great compassion for the animal, but the owner refused to have it treated. When the farmer left the barn, Mr. Herriott injected it with enough nembutal to put it painlessly to sleep. After a few days, he returned to the farm at the owner's request and saw the sheep standing in her stall. He inquired as to whether or not it was the same beast who, a few days earlier, had been at death's door. The farmer assured him that it was, that she had slept for two days, and that he was amazed the animal was still alive. The vet was so astounded, knowing the poor animal should have died from the injection. The conclusion he reached after trying the same experiment on another sick animal was that the medication had induced a period of total rest for the animal—a period in which her body was allowed to heal and regain its strength. A proper balance in our lives will allow our bodies to rest when they are tired and a time of convalescence when they are sick.

Smile and laugh. Have a kind word for someone everyday. Meet problems head on. Set goals and achieve them. Make a schedule and stick to it. Get busy and work hard. Learn to relax when you should, and, above all, get right with God. This can only be accomplished through prayer and study. If you don't know the teachings of Jesus, how can you possibly live by them? Know what's in the Bible!

David and Bathsheba

A classic example of depression brought about by grief and pain is recorded in II Samuel 11 and 12. David was king of Israel. Everything was at his disposal. One day while walking on the roof of his palace, he saw a woman bathing. His lust consumed him, and he ordered that she be brought to his chamber. There they committed adultery.

The beautiful Bathsheba has a less than perfect reputation due to this act, but when you consider *who* David was, she probably responded like anyone else would have under the circumstances. After all, he was *the king*.

The sequence of events which follows this adulterous union is preposterous, eventually leading to the death of Bathsheba's husband at the hands of the king. The pair married and obviously David thought his attempt to conceal his sin had been successful. "But the thing that David had done displeased the Lord" (II Samuel 11:27, KJV).

So the Lord sent Nathan to convict David of his sin. Following a stinging rebuke, the prophet told the king that what he had done had all been in secret but the Lord's reprisals against David would be out in the open for all of Israel to see. David admitted, "I have sinned against the Lord," and he suffered great sorrow over the death of his and Bathsheba's child.

The wonderful thing about David's depression is his recovery. No doubt he bore the scars of his sins throughout his lifetime, but in the New Testament we see his unique place in God's plan for the Savior of the world, "That Christ cometh of the seed of David. . . ." (John 7:42, KJV).

Also, David is described as a man after God's own heart (Acts 13:22). In his affair with Bathsheba, he had sunk about as low as any man can—deceitful, manipulative, adulterous, murderous, but still God was willing to forgive him. David repented and once again became the Lord's servant. Here again we see the second chance given by the Father to His obedient, repenting child. No matter how useless our lives may seem, God is always there. He will never give up on us. In turn, we should never give up on ourselves.

Chapter Ten

1. Why is it important for us to be mentally well-balanced? What about phobias?
2. What role does God play in mental illness?
3. What is your attitude toward depression and other mental disorders? Can one look to you for guidance and support?
4. How does sin affect our mental capabilities? What part does conscience play in mental stability?
5. Recall others in the scriptures who suffered from depression.
6. List the different agencies in your community where one can go for help in combating mental problems. Which ones do you consider good, which ones bad. Why?

CHAPTER 11

Invisible Sins, Invisible Rewards

The thought comes to mind that perhaps an entire book could be written on the subject of invisible sins—those trepasses to which we like to refer as "little" and we try so hard to keep hidden from the eyes of others. They are mostly crimes of the heart, inward sins known primarily to us. Often the transgression goes unchecked for years, perhaps from neglect or ignorance on the part of the guilty party, or even the refusal of the sinner to recognize and correct the wrongdoing.

Every sin we commit originates in the heart and comes out of the body spewing defilement along its path.

> That which cometh out of the man, that defileth the man. For from within, out of the heart of men, proceed evil thoughts, adulteries, fornications, murders, thefts, covetousness, wickedness, deceit, lasciviousness, and evil eye, blasphemy, pride, foolishness: All these things come from within, and defile the man (Mark 7:20-23, KJV).

A $100 dollar bill could be placed on my desk at work, and if it should lie there for a year, I would never take it or use it for my own benefit. Why? Because I am not a thief. I do not steal. Neither do I lie, not even a little white lie. That truth came home to me very poignantly as a girl when I became entrapped in a half-truth involving a question put to me by my mother. That little bit of lying weighed upon my consciousness for approximately twenty-four hours until my guilt-ridden conscience finally corrected its error.

Lying, stealing, and cheating pose no problem for me. However, there are some invisible sins which continually plague me. I know where my weaknesses are and I must constantly guard against Satan's attempts to control my life in these areas. You, too, have invisible sins. To recognize your faults is not a weakness. Real weakness is the failure to correct those faults.

Just as we made the list of the most important things in our lives, we need also to compile a list of danger spots. When temptations come, as they surely will, our very best defenses must be deployed to ward them off. In our study here, we cannot possibly deal with all the invisible sins, but we will touch on several of them. As you study, do so with a child's heart, ever striving to please your Father in heaven.

The Invisible Sins and Their Antidotes

1—Envy (Contentment)

Envy is one of those wicked little sins which often causes more pain for the one envious than the recipient. Webster says that envy is "a feeling of discontent and ill will because of another's advantages, possessions, etc.: resentful dislike of another who has something desirable."

To be envious is to be carnally minded (I Corinthians 3:3). It often causes hurt feelings and a desire on the part of the envious one for terrible disaster to befall the more privileged. Often we feel it's perfectly alright for a person to have their advantages, but we feel badly because we can't have the same "perks".

Envy often surfaces over the most innocent thing and at a most unsuspecting time. For me, envy comes in the form of beautiful homes and tall trees in well-established yards. Because of my great love of nature, I would give almost anything to plant a tree and watch it grow for twenty years. Several trees have gone into the ground and been nurtured, but never have I seen one of them grow to maturity.

Since moving to West Texas, however, I have discovered that families in the oil business move more often than ministers. One lady related that she and her family had moved twelve times in thirteen years, and had actually lived in one place for only two and one half years. Some of the moves were not promotional, only lateral, resulting in no financial gain.

Personally, envy is at the top of my list. My envious feelings may seem petty at first, but let's look at some other things of which we can become envious. Are you envious of another's car, jewelry, or mink coat? Quite possibly, it's someone's position (job), or status in the community. Perhaps it is their popularity, the success of their children versus the success of your own children, their talents, or their money. Isn't it ridiculous to be jealous of any of these things? Envy is *petty!* There is no gain in it, only discontentment. It's like a cancer slowly gnawing away at the good in a woman's life.

A sound heart is the life of the flesh: but envy the rottenness of the bones (Proverbs 14:30, KJV).

The NIV says it this way:

A heart at peace gives life to the body, but envy rots the bones. In this verse, we see the cure for envy—a heart at peace. In Hebrews 13:5, the writer admonishes us to "be content with such things as ye have." The apostle Paul had learned to be content in whatever situation he found himself (Phillipians 4:11). The imagery here is one of self-containment. We make of our lives either a prison or a palace. If our wants and desires control us then we become prisoners to our own lusts. But if we shape our lives after Jesus' principles and not after envious thoughts cast in another's direction, we will have peace of heart and contentment.

2—Covetousness (Greed) and a Generous Heart

Covetousness and greed are so closely tied together that it is almost impossible to separate one from the other.

Basically, the problem here is desiring something so badly that it becomes an inordinate obsession. "Such is the end of all who go after ill-gotten gain: it takes away the lives of those who get it" (Proverbs 1:19, NIV). Rather than being greedy, the Lord would have us to cultivate a generous spirit that is always willing to share with others.

> Remember this: Whoever sows sparingly will also reap sparingly, and whosoever sows generously will also reap generously. Each man should give what he has decided in his heart to give not reluctantly or under compulsion, for God loves a cheerful giver (II Corinthians 9:6,7, NIV).

When the Lord starts measuring out our blessings we don't want Him to use a teaspoon. "With the same measure that ye mete withal it shall be measured to you again" (Luke 6:38, KJV). He'll use the same container to measure our blessings as we use when dealing with our brothers and sisters in Christ and the people of the world. If we are generous and gracious, then God will be the same with us. If we are tight and stingy, He will be the same with us. Bring on the *dumptruck*, oh Lord!

3—Fibbing and Whispering (Honor and Integrity)

Lying and gossip go hand in hand. You just might be able to discern if a person is a gossip, but it's truly harder to tell if someone is a liar. This is particularly difficult if an individual is an accomplished liar. Some will even lie when it would be easier to tell the truth. The discouraging part of this problem is that more and more Christians—teenagers and adults—lie as a matter of course, not giving any heed to the Scriptures regarding this sin.

There are seven things which the Lord hates, and a lying tongue is one of them (Proverbs 6:16,17). If the Lord hates lying, we certainly do not need to have any part in it.

Why does someone lie? No matter what reason is given, to cover up a deed or to protect someone's feelings, a woman lies because she wants to hurt someone or be deceitful. "A lying tongue hates those it hurts and a flattering mouth works ruin" (Proverbs 26:28, NIV).

Why does one talk about others? Why do we possess a need to know everything about everyone and then proceed to tell it? This is a way of building ourselves up in the sight of others. If we know a lot of facts—especially juicy personal tidbits about others—we can demand another's attention while the gossip is spread. The cruelest aspect of gossip is that it has no redeeming quality. It only assists in the tearing down of another person's life.

> Do not let any unwholesome talk come out of your mouths, but only what is helpful for building others up according to their needs, that it may benefit those who listen (Ephesians 4:29, NIV).

The simple truth is that if one lies or gossips, she cannot be trusted. If she lies to others, she will lie to you. If she gossips about others to you, she will gossip about you to others. Examine your own manner of speech and your motives. Do you talk too much about others? Are you guilty of causing unrest and divisions among your sisters in Christ by evil sayings? Absorb, but don't tell. We are not each others enemies. Don't wound the body with idle talk.

"Better is the poor that walketh in his integrity, than he that is perverse in his lips and is a fool" (Proverbs 19:1, KJV). For some reason we have gotten away from the idea that a woman's word is her bond, that what she says and does is what counts. Where have all the honorable women gone? I for one hope there is a revival of the spirit of integrity among Christian women. It is so badly needed.

4—Hatred (Forgiveness)

A knot of nausea and bitterness tightened its grip in the woman's stomach at the sound of her once dear friend's voice. Previously very close, an unresolved misunderstanding desperately threatened their relationship.

We've all had the experience. Nothing hurts worse than

a friend turning her back on you. That pain is doubled if the friend is a Christian.

I once spoke to a woman who had become embroiled in a nasty dispute with a sister in Christ. Upon admonishing her to resolve the situation, she curtly replied, "It's not worth it."

Our human side harbors ill will toward others, and in this behavior Satan has found one of his most powerful tools. It's very easy for a disgruntled person to completely disregard verses like "By this shall all men know ye are my disciples, if ye love one another" (John 13:35, KJV). Obviously, the worth of working through one's differences with another is an individual's soul.

The process of forgiveness is rarely explained. We only know that we are to forgive if we are to be forgiven by our Lord (Matthew 6:14). How then do we forgive anyone anything the way Jesus commanded? This simple formula is easy to follow and always successful.

First, recognize that the problem of bitterness and strife lies within you. If you hate someone, feel wronged or hurt by her behavior, talk to God. He *already* knows what is in our hearts, so confess your emotions freely in prayer (Philippians 4:6). Release pent-up anguish and pain and realize that you are indeed capable of getting rid of your hatred.

Second, once in the morning and again at night, pray for the person who has abused or shunned you.

> Love your enemies, bless them that curse you, do good to them that hate you, and pray for them which despitefully use you, and persecute you (Matthew 5:44, KJV).

Call the culprit by name. Ask God to bless him or her. Pray for her physical and spiritual welfare. Initially, you may choke on the person's name and feel hypocritical, but after a period of just two weeks, there will be a remarkable change in *your* attitude. It is extremely difficult to hate someone for whom you are actively and earnestly praying.

Last of all and by far the most difficult, confront the person face to face.

> Moreover if thy brother shall trespass against thee, go and tell him his fault between thee and him alone: if he shall hear thee, thou has gained thy brother (Matthew 18:15, KJV).

If you are at fault, confess, saying, "I'm sorry, I've hurt you." Just remember, the responsibility is always yours to correct the problem.

> Therefore, if thou bring thy gift to the altar, and there rememberest that thy brother hath ought against thee: Leave there thy gift before the altar, and go thy way; first be reconciled to thy brother, and then come and offer thy gift (Matthew 5:23,24, KJV).

We'll never be able to like everyone, but a Christian cannot hate anyone. Hatred is as foreign to the nature of Jesus Christ as salt is to drinking water. Get the problem out in the open and let it air. Remember, if you do not forgive, you will not be forgiven. Heed the warning!

5—Compromise (Faithfulness)

Compromise is possibly the worst of all invisible sins. When we take on the attitude of indifference, nothing matters anymore. There is no right or wrong, no justice or injustice, no good or evil. No one takes a stand for righteousness.

Compromise with evil is a crippler, preventing God's people from doing His will. Compromise is a killer of reason clouding our sensibilities concerning the great dangers associated with Satan. Compromise presents such a great threat because it takes away our ability to be distinguished as part of the kingdom of our dear Lord (Titus 2:14). The pure truth of Jesus Christ should never be placed on the same level with any other man's teachings because his thoughts came from God (John 10:25).

The list of invisible sins could go on and on. It includes

such thing as fear, worry, high-mindedness, prejudice, and strife. Your weakness may not be found here, but don't be deceived. Your sin does not go unnoticed by God. Be certain there is no hypocrisy where He is concerned. We must guard against the wiles of Satan in order to reach heaven.

Invisible Rewards

It is ingrained in our nature to seek praise for our accomplishments. We cook a special dinner and expect our families to rave about it. Our good deeds should be recognized above anyone else's. We are not unlike those Pharisees of old who stood on the street corners in their finest robes uttering profound prayers so that everyone who passed by could say, "Look at him. Isn't he great!" (Matthew 6:5, 23:1-7).

Our Lord is rewarding His children now and He will continue to do so forever. The promise for some of our reward is given in Matthew 6. Jesus admonishes us to do our service in secret and God will reward us. Secret service is the hardest, because it carries with it little or no chance of praise from anyone except perhaps the recipient and God. The bestowing of glory may not come now, but later.

Our life must be one of service to Jesus and to our fellowman. It's hard for us to be servants because we want to be served. But Jesus said, "My father will honor the one who serves me" (John 12:26, NIV). Jesus came to serve, and we must imitate Him. His entire life was one of service, and His ultimate sacrifice revealed His great love for us.

A Challenge

Commit to a project of service for the period of one year. This project will not cost any money and very little of your time. Pick out one person, perhaps someone you genuinely have trouble getting along with or someone with a burden. Once everyday, mention this person to God. Pray for them, calling them by name. Tell no one else for whom you are praying. Just watch the invisible rewards come your way. The person will grow to be your friend, you'll feel responsible for the good in her life because of your prayers, and you'll be richly rewarded, invisibly, by our Father.

Chapter Eleven

1. Why are we so reluctant to admit to secret sins?
2. Why is it important for the Christian not to have concealed sins in her life?
3. Discuss the "Dorain Gray" concept of sin in our lives.
4. What is the best possible way for a Christian to avoid sin?
5. List some positive steps in leading a more pure life.

CHAPTER 12

Accepting The Unacceptable

A Man With Real Problems

One day the sons of God (angels) came to present themselves before the Lord, and Satan came in with them. He had been roaming the earth so God asked him, "Have you considered my servant Job? There is no one on earth like him; he is blameless and upright, a man who fears God and shuns evil" (Job 1:8, NIV). Satan accused God of putting a hedge around Job, blessing him far beyond what anyone could imagine. "Stretch out your hand and strike everything he has, and he will surely curse you to your face," Satan said (v. 11). The Lord had faith in Job and so allowed Satan to take away all of his possessions, including his beloved sons and daughters.

Later, on another day, God's sons and Satan came into the presence of Jehovah. The Lord once again praised Job's integrity. We do not know how much time had elapsed since Satan had first plagued Job, but we do know that he had been suffering grief for whatever length of time it had been. Satan reminded God, "A man will give all he has for his own life" (Job 2:4, NIV). The Lord consented to let Satan touch Job, but he could not take his life. Satan afflicted the poor man even more with sore boils from his head to his feet. They were so painful that Job sat down in ashes and scraped himself with a broken piece of pottery. He was indeed a miserable man.

Job had some major problems, the biggest of which was that God had allowed Satan to have him. In the New Testament, the devil also asked to have Simon Peter, to shake him as chaff in the wind, but Jesus said, "I have prayed for you, Simon, that your faith may not fail" (Luke 22:32, NIV). It's scary to think that Satan may also have asked for us.

Job suffered loss of property and wealth and loved ones. How grieved he must have been when his own wife foolishly encouraged him to curse God and die (Job 2:9). She, too, had suffered—the deaths of her children, her great wealth and esteem gone, and now her husband of no use to her in his pitiable condition. And if all of this weren't enough, Job's friends turned against him, falsely accusing him of wrongdoing. How much more could Job and his wife be expected to bear?

In contrast to Job, we have in the New Testament, the story of Martha, Mary and Lazarus' sister. In Luke 10, Martha was in a dither when Mary left her alone to prepare a meal for Jesus all by herself. Many chose instead to sit at the Master's feet and learn all she could from Him. The Lord rebuked Martha because her priorities were not in their proper place. He reminded her that "Mary has chose what is better and it will not be taken away from her" (v. 42).

Job had real problems. Martha only thought she did. Most of our problems are exaggerated and more importance given to them than they deserve. Martha's bickering over "supposed" problems is a good example. These little, nagging problems consume so much of our thoughts that we waste precious time and energy worrying over them. We could instead devote that time to overcoming the real hardships in our lives. Let's look at some of the major problems we may be called upon to face during our lifetimes.

1—Death

The ultimate challenge of anyone's life is death. But death need not be a fearful expectation for the Christian. There are many things worse than dying. One of those things is not being ready to die. Every man has an appointment with death, from this there is no escape (Hebrews 9:27). After death comes judgment. If we are going to have any fear, it should be of judgment. But fear brings torment. We are told there is no fear in the love of God (I John 4:18).

In this was manifested the love of God toward us, because that God sent his only begotten Son into the world that we might live through him. Herein is love, not that we loved God, but that he loved us, and sent his Son to be the propitiation for our sins (I John 4:9,10, KJV).

Our love for God and His Son should cast all fear about the hereafter from our hearts.

And this is the record, that God hath given to us eternal life, and this life is in his Son. He that hath the Son hath life; and he that hath not the Son of God hath not life. These things have I written unto you that believe on the name of the Son of God: that ye may know that ye have eternal life, and that ye may believe on the name of the Son (I John 4:11-13, KJV).

We can know that our future is secure with God through a knowledge of His Son and a dedication to His will.

2—The Lord Giveth and Taketh Away

When Job lost his possessions he said, "Naked came I out of my mother's womb and naked shall I return thither: the Lord gave and the Lord hath taken away; blessed be the name of the Lord" (Job 1:21, KJV). Job was mistaken about his misfortune. The Lord had blessed him with his many herds and fine sons and daughters, but *Satan* took them away. The minute disaster befalls us, we ask, "Why did the Lord let this happen?" We know that every good and perfect gift comes from God (James 1:17), but where does the bad originate?

Let no man say when he is tempted: I am tempted of God: for God cannot be tempted with evil; neither tempteth he any man: But every man is tempted when he is drawn away of his own lust and enticed (James 1:13,14, KJV).

The NIV says it even plainer:

> When tempted, no one should say, "God is tempting me." For God cannot be tempted by evil, nor does he tempt anyone; but each one is tempted when, by his own evil desire, he is dragged away and enticed.

We must not be deceived. Satan is a real being, walking about seeking whom he may devour (I Peter 5:8). In the form of our material possessions—those creature comforts which cushion us and bring us great power—he has found a base to attack us at the very foundation of our souls. Take away our cars, houses, jobs, and children, and the poor helpless human will crumble. That's why we are not to put our faith and trust in the things upon the earth.

> Do not store up for yourselves treasures on earth, where moth and rust destroy, and where thieves break in and steal. But store up for yourselves treasures in heaven, where moth and rust do not destroy and where thieves do not break in and steal. For where your treasure is, there your heart will be also (Matthew 6:19,20,21, NIV).

Our security in life comes from the Lord not our bank accounts. The earth will pass away but our trust in God will endure.

3—Divorce

A friend was separated from her husband when they were both very young. With a small child to raise, she contemplated her bleak future. The love she possessed for her husband could not overcome his bad behavior, and their constant fighting had driven her from their home. Finally, one day she assessed the situation. As she saw it, she had three options. She could stay away from her husband and seek a divorce, go back to him and live with the arguing and bickering, or go back and live in peace. She chose the latter. She returned home, learned to control her temper, prayed for guidance and sought peace. This couple recently celebrated their twentieth-fifth wedding anniversary. It was only achieved by a mellowing of her attitude.

Divorce is a stinging defeat for any woman. The rejection and the loss is often overwhelming. Great faith in God is sometimes the only thing that will see a person through this difficult situation. But divorce is not the end of a person's life. A woman must pick up the pieces and continue on.

In the state of Texas, there is a very strange law regarding divorce. There is no alimony. A judge decides how to split a couple's assets, usually 50-50, so there can be no dependency of a wife upon her ex-husband after the dissolution of their marriage. Under these circumstances, a woman finds she must be able and willing to stand on her own if she is to provide for herself and her children as well, since child-support is usually very difficult, if not impossible, to collect.

4—Illness

Years ago, my husband was in a motorcycle club, and on one occasion visited another member's home. After ringing the doorbell, the friend's wife appeared at the door. Having introduced himself, my husband heard this reply, "My name is ____________________, and I've just had bladder surgery." A sick person needs sympathy, but not pity. A sick person needs someone to say, "I understand. I'm here."

Unfortunately for some of us, our lot in life will be to suffer pain. We will have no choice in the matter. Medical science will be unable to intervene on our behalf, and our lives will end in excruciating pain. I had the privilege to sit with a very sick woman one week prior to her death. Her abdomen was filled with cancerous tumors, some even bursting through previous surgical incisions for more space in which to grow. She patiently accepted her lot, awaiting death, enduring the unrelenting pain. The night of her death, the doctor praised her heroic attitude to her husband. "I cannot understand how she endured so much pain without going mad," he said. Her wise Christian husband explained it to him. She trusted Jesus Christ. She knew the horrors inside her body would soon end her existence on this earth, but she would then live with God forever.

We do not know what is to befall us in the area of health. Some are blessed with extremely long lives that are free from pain, while others endure it constantly and are never free from its grip. Paul begged the Lord to remove his thorn in the flesh, but the Lord refused saying, "My grace is sufficient for thee: for my strength is made perfect in weakness" (II Corinthians 12:9, KJV). Look at Paul's life. He endured the torment and pressed on in the cause of Christ, never letting his infirmities interfere with his work. "Most gladly therefore will I rather glory in my infirmities, that the power of Christ may rest upon me" (II Corinthians 12:9, KJV). Being ill does not affect our relationship with God, except that it sometimes makes us more dependent upon Him for strength, which we do not feel we need when we are whole.

The Myth

There is a widely circulated myth which many Christians believe, and which is highly touted by several in the religious world. The concept is this:

"Because we are Christians, everything will go well with us. If we are good, live a *righteous* life, God will protect us from trouble (i.e., illness, disease, disaster). If our faith in God is strong enough, we will not have to suffer."

Job was a righteous man. There was none other like him in the whole world, but he had to suffer. Suffering has everything to do with righteousness. In fact, we are promised "all that live godly in Christ Jesus shall suffer persecution" (II Timothy 3:12, KJV). Paul said, "for Christ's sake, I delight in weaknesses, in insults, in hardships, in persecutions, in difficulties. For when I am weak, then I am strong" (II Corinthians 12:10, NIV).

Our concept of happiness is a life free from thorns, but it's the thorns of life that help us develop character and give us hope in God's promise of a more tranquil atmosphere in which to spend eternity. "We must go through many hardships to enter the kingdom of God" (Acts 14:22, NIV).

Life is like an elevator: up and down, up and down, filled with mometary setbacks coupled with periods of euphoric bliss. Some things can be changed, worked out. Others can't. Problems become either a crisis or a challenge. We are either weighed down under their load or motivated to greater heights of achievement. Some problems may never be solved, and there may be no ending to their existence. But never think more of your troubles than you do your blessings.

Tiffany is three years old. She and her father were getting ready to go out when she asked him how long it would be before they left. "About ten minutes," he replied. She thought for a moment and then asked, "How long is ten minutes, Daddy?" Realizing that Tiffany had no concept of time, her father answered, "Just a short time." With God things work out over a period of time, but we impatiently seek an immediate solution to our problems. We don't walk by faith, but rather by sight. We want, and often need, to see the end up ahead.

But God has promised, "Blessed is the man who preserveres under trial, because when he has stood the test, he will receive the crown of life that God has promised to those who love him" (James 1:12, NIV). Henry Nouwen says in his book *The Wounded Healer,* "The great illusion of leadership is to think that we can be led out of the desert by someone who has never been there." Christ has been there—to the cross, suffering, dying, and committing Himself to God's eternal purpose. He is our example, our role model in learning to accept the unacceptable.

Chapter Twelve

1. Woman wants her life to be perfect. Discuss why?
2. Do trials and tribulations lessen one in the sight of others? Why do we not always show compassion to those in distress?
3. Where can we go for help in overcoming our problems? Discuss the role of the Holy Spirit in supporting the Christian.
4. When God has made a final decision regarding our problem, are we able to accept his verdict (solution)?

CHAPTER 13

AH! Woman

We've come to the last chapter. Writing a book isn't easy. There were a couple of reasons why I even dared try it. In the first place, it seemed like an enormous challenge, and I wanted to see if I could actually put a book together. Second, I hoped to share common ideas and goals with other women of like faith.

Actually, we are like books with a new page written each day in the history of our lives. Some pages are more glorious than others, some days more appealing, some more beautiful. I am now forty years old. At this age, life is both challenging and bewildering. It's a time to pause and reflect upon what has already transpired in the last four decades—to contemplate the successes achieved, to look back with sadness and humor at the failures, and to accept the imperfections that inevitably come with everyone's life. It is also a time to look forward with expectation and anticipation to what lies ahead.

One of life's greatest surprises is that the older we get, the more we know. This is not true with everyone, but if a woman remains open with a willingness to learn, she can and will gain new knowledge everyday. This is why it is also important to study God's word. My father-in-law reads the New Testament through, on a regular schedule, about thirteen times a year, and steadfastly maintains he learns something new every time he does so. There are three important things I *know* at forty which I could not comprehend at thirty. They are:

1—God loves me.

2—I am a worthy person made in the image of the Lord.

3—Jesus Christ is the way.

These facts are especially interesting when you consider that I was reared in a Christian home with devout Christian parents. I guess we were so concerned about what to do and what not to do, we never seemed to get down to the *real* gospel.

Growth

In God's world, growth is permissible. We come into God's kingdom as babies, not knowing much more than how to crawl, and desiring "the sincere milk of the word" (I Peter 2:2, KJV). We are not perfect when we come to God. If we were, there would be no need for Christ's blood of atonement. Instead, we take turns with God—He gives to us and we give to Him. He gave us a way of escape from sin and degradation. All He asks in return is our total love and devotion.

What the student must realize is that the attainment of the goal is not immediate. Instead it is a gradual process, often by trial and error, of learning God's desires for us. Think of your Christian life as a graph with the word "Salvation" written across it. The graph line may go up and down representing your spirituals highs and lows, but it is never permitted to become a flat line. A flat line indicates no growth. It is only by learning and doing that the love of God grows in us to develop mature Christians. However, we could save ourselves a great deal of heartache at the outset if we would only listen to the Holy Spirit through the inspired words of God in the first place. Don't wait until you fail to read the instruction booklet.

We must never let our own arrogance concerning our relationship with God falsely cloud the true condition of our soul. Our guard should always be extended to protect ourselves from Satan and his followers. Christians should not be lulled into a sense of security by sitting back on their past laurels thinking God expects nothing else from them. We were "created in Christ Jesus to do good works, which God prepared in advance for us to do" (Ephesians 2:10, NIV).

In II Thessalonians 2, the apostle Paul admonishes these Christians to stay alert, because if one did not receive the truth, "God shall send them strong delusion, that they should believe a lie: That they all might be damned who believed not the truth, but had pleasure in unrighteousness" (v. 11-12). God will give us up if we do not do His will. It's as simple as that. But He will not give up on us as long as we are striving, with pure hearts, to be His children. It is the commitment that counts.

The War

There's a very bitter and very tragic war going on in the world. Oh, it's not being waged with nuclear bombs or heat-seeking missiles, nor in the "cold" diplomacy surrounding a bargaining table. The final outcome of this war has already been determined. All that's left to be decided is the body count, or should we say the *soul* count.

Sin is still in the world as evidenced in James 2:10 and James 4:17. It is a *real* part of a *real* world. In Romans 3:9-19, the writer gives us a stinging essay about sin and some of its complications. It is of the greatest importance that we realize sin is here with us, that our lives can be wrecked by it, and that we have to separate ourselves from it with the utmost speed.

Christ has won the battle! "But thanks be to God, which giveth us the victory through our Lord Jesus Christ" (I Corinthians 15:57, KJV). Also, "The Lord works out everything for his own ends, even the wicked for a day of disaster" (Proverbs 16:4, NIV). But Satan is on a tear. He just will not give up until judgment. He wants to drag as many helpless souls down with him to hell as he possibly can.

Then what is the solution? How can we escape the clutches of damnation? The solution is found in I John 1:7, "But if we walk in the light, as he is in the light, we have fellowship with one another, and the blood of Jesus, his Son, purifies us from all sin" (NIV). The original Greek word here indicates a *continual* cleansing as long as we are in the light. What a comforting thought! *Jesus Christ is the solution!* He and God are not dead. They are still at work.

Jesus said Himself in John 5:17, "My Father is always at his work to this very day, and I, too, am working" (NIV). The Jews wanted to murder him for saying that, but to the Christian it proves that our heavenly protectors care about us and what happens to us. God's will is being done. He is in charge, and in this we can have hope, "Looking for that blessed hope and the glorious appearing of the great God and our Savior Jesus Christ" (Titus 2:13, KJV).

Take a Stand

Now is the time for the Christians of the world to be counted. We sing that old song "Stand Up For Jesus" but some of us long ago forgot what we were standing for. We have reached a period in our lives where things are no longer black or white, good or evil. Everything is gray—the color of compromise—an in-between color of mediocrity. Gone are the days when someone's word was bond, a handshake more binding than any words written in a contract.

Jesus was a man of *integrity!* Truthful, honest, hard-working, and loyal unto God. Through His teachings, we can find peace. "And the peace of God, which passeth all understanding, shall keep your hearts and minds through Christ Jesus" (Phillipians 4:7, KJV).

The Psalmist said, "Turn my eyes away from worthless

things, renew my life according to your word" (Psalms 119:37, NIV). Life is like a high-tension basketball game that comes down to the last few seconds before the buzzer sounds. You win some and you lose some, but the winners in this life deal in determination, integrity, positive thinking, and in the confidence that God keeps His promises. "I will never leave thee, nor forsake thee" (Hebrews 13:5 KJV).

Use every experience for growth. Learn from everything. If you're weighed down and oppressed by your seeming religious devotion you're struggling against Jesus and God.

The things that count haven't changed. My grandmother's life was structured and ordered. She followed a set routine everyday with little if any variation. Even my parents rarely attended a party without their children in tow. We hardly ever had a babysitter. But circumstances have changed. The mobility of our society has caused change, and with this rapid change has come progress. But is it real progress? The world is not necessarily "better" now than it was a hundred years ago. We still have pain and suffering, death and destruction, wars, and famine.

The only stability we have is in the treasure that Christ left us: love, sharing, giving, responding to others' needs, devotion to family, and adoration of God. A severe sense of loss accompanies the absence of God from our lives. There are no shortcuts in dealing with God, only hard work, self-discipline, and devotion are permissible. Succeeding is not hard. It is the attempting that is difficult. If we are to be successful in our relationship with God, we must be diligently seeking Him (Hebrews 11:6).

The Final Stroke

Ah, woman! Winsome and comely, soft and warm. Men have sailed round the world seeking your favor. Cities and nations have been built and destroyed on a whim to please you. Your beauty and grace have been poured out onto the written page in poetic verse.

Behold, thou art fair, my love:
Behold, thou art fair; thou hast doves' eyes
Behold, thou art fair, my beloved, yea pleasant;
also, our bed is green (Song of Solomon 1:15-17, KJV)

Woman should strive to be like Jesus as He came to serve, not to be served; to minister, not be ministered unto. A woman's birthright is to serve. Has it ever occurred to you that in a moment of service, you might be the answer to someone's problem? That through your good works and Christian attitude, you just might lead someone to Jesus? That it might only be through you that a person ever comes to a knowledge of the truth? In this divine scope, a simple prayer can be uttered:

"Benevolent Father, help me to do my best, and help me to be like Jesus."

There is great risk in loving mortals. One can be faced with rejection or indifference. A once intimate relationship can turn sour. But in God's family there is only care and concern.

What do you think? If a man own a hundred sheep, and one of them wanders away, will he not leave the ninety-nine on the hills and go to look for the one that wandered off? And if he finds it, I tell you the truth, he is happier about that one sheep than about the ninety-nine that did not wander off. In the same way your Father in heaven is not willing that any of these little ones should be lost (Matthew 18:12-14, NIV).

The Good Shepherd knows His sheep, "and the sheep listen to his voice. He calls his own sheep by name and leads them out. When he has brought out all his own he goes on ahead of them, and his sheep follow because they know his voice" (John 10:3,4, NIV).

Does Christ know your name?

Chapter Thirteen

1. What are some of the new things you have learned about God as you have grown older?
2. Do you feel that you are progressing in God's kingdom or going backwards? Discuss your reasons for your answer.
3. Are you convinced that Satan is real and alive. Why?
4. Why is integrity such an important trait to develop?
5. Are you living up to your birthright of service? List the ways you are serving God.